THE CREATIVE WORKFORCE

Professor Erica McWilliam is an internationally recognised author in the field of education, with a particular focus on workforce preparation of youth in post-compulsory schooling and higher education. Her research and scholarship spans the entire spectrum of learning, from early years to doctoral education. She is also an author and social commentator on corporate practice.

THE CREATIVE WORKFORCE

HOW TO LAUNCH YOUNG PEOPLE INTO HIGH-FLYING FUTURES

Erica McWilliam

UNSW
PRESS

To Crocket, who has such a wonderful future,
and to Isaac, whose future was taken away.

A UNSW Press book
Published by
University of New South Wales Press Ltd
University of New South Wales
Sydney NSW 2052
Australia
www.unswpress.com.au

National Library of Australia
Cataloguing-in-Publication entry
Author: McWilliam, Erica.
Title: The creative workforce: how to launch young people into high-flying futures/
        Erica McWilliam.
ISBN: 978 1 921410 22 2 (pbk.)
Notes: Includes index.
Subjects: Education – Curricula – Australia
        Teaching – Australia.
        Creative ability – Australia.
        Creative ability in business – Australia.
Dewey Number: 658.3140994

Design Josephine Pajor-Markus
Cover istock
Printer Ligare

This book is printed on paper using fibre supplied from plantation or sustainably
managed forests.

FSC
Mixed Sources
Product group from well-managed
forests and other controlled sources
Cert no. SGS-COC-004233
www.fsc.org
© 1996 Forest Stewardship Council

Contents

Foreword

We live in a time of immense and accelerating change. We work in a consumer age where the refocus of education towards economic ends is interwoven with discourses of excellence, performance enhancement, efficiency and effectiveness of the workforce. We live and work in response to education policies that mandate rapid change, driven by tables, tests and targets. Added to this is the imperative, convincingly argued in this groundbreaking book, to prepare young people for fast-changing work futures.

Using empirical research, primary source information, and narratives enhanced by poetry, vignettes and other insightful nuggets that go beyond traditional disciplinary boundaries, Erica McWilliam makes a compelling case for a world where classrooms, as well as boardrooms, become the places to demonstrate the courage necessary for developing ways of understanding educational improvement. *The Creative Workforce* presents key debates with solutions for all – whether as teach-

ers, politicians, policy-makers, parents, business managers or students
– who need to engage in the radical rethinking necessary to develop
new ways of understanding and effecting change.

Erica McWilliam calls us to think long and hard about the changing nature of work and our work futures. In every chapter, we are
invited, and, indeed, assisted, to unpack our assumptions about the
kinds of skills and capacities, dispositions and expertise that will enable
generations of young people to achieve their goals in a competitive
global labour market. It will be of interest to all who want to develop
the creative potential of young people.

In *The Creative Workforce* Erica McWilliam emerges as one of the
world's leading scholars on creativity as it relates to education systems
and workplaces. McWilliam is a consummate storyteller; a sure-handed
guide who moves beyond the old debates about creativity to configure
new learning cultures in education. This book develops a new way of
understanding educational improvement.

Erica McWilliam sheds light on the trends, values and thinking
of 'today's kids' in terms of what they learn, how they learn and who
they learn most from in the changing world of 21st-century work. She
invites us to think about issues globally and locally, and from many
disciplinary perspectives in ways that challenge consensual views of
creativity. In this way, Erica ventures further than previous writers on
creativity.

She confronts some of the myths of education we have cherished
for too long and calls upon us to think critically, politically and strategically. She advises both teachers and policy-makers on the need to
develop new forms of pedagogical practice in order to build creative
capacity in their students.

This book raises questions about 'what counts' as education and
frames creativity in education as a dynamic human enterprise that
entails the nurture of risk-taking as an essential means of learning to
learn. In this, McWilliam describes and synthesises what we need to
know about how to cultivate, nurture and assess creativity.

In a time when workplace dilemmas mean 'creativity' is constantly
coming under scrutiny from those who demand certainty rather than

uncertainty, predictability rather than unpredictability, how satisfying it is to read a book that challenges this view. Most importantly, this author helps us, in vivid and contextualised ways, to realise our own enquiry as change agents. This emphasises reflection upon choices and consideration of the consequences of action or nonaction.

The Creative Workforce will be essential reading for anyone involved in education, policy-making, school improvement and effectiveness, including academics, educators, researchers, head teachers, advisers, community workers, business managers and parents. This book is appropriate for use in the schools and universities and the larger community. It will ask you to think positively and afresh about change and about our experiential understanding of our workplace.

Pamela Burnard, University of Cambridge, UK

Acknowledgments

This book would not have been possible without my fabulous flock-mates. Shane Dawson has been a major source of new ideas, fresh information, close editing, warm friendship and unfailing optimism. Peter Taylor is as ever the greatest partner a woman could have, respectful, loving and a deep believer in dialogue. Jen Tan is a one-woman dynamo who is invariably smart, efficient, ebullient and always up-beat. Ruth Bridgstock is multitalented, agile, generous and a seriously smart data analyst. Sandra Haukka is capable and loyal, and committed to supporting any and every effort to build the work of the team.

I also want to acknowledge the great collegiality of Dr Don Lebler and Professor Paul Draper at the Queensland Conservatorium of Music, and my colleagues Professor Greg Hearn, Professor Stuart Cunningham and Professor John Hartley in the Faculty of Creative Industries at the Queensland University of Technology. Thank you all.

Introduction

This book is about preparing young people for exciting futures – for living, learning and earning more productively. I have written it because this is a crucial issue for educators and employers, parents and policy-makers alike. With mounting criticisms of the formal education and training that our young people are currently receiving, we need to know more about the value of what they are learning and whether their formal education really is adequate to their future needs.

Our institutions may well be failing to deliver a 21st-century education, but I am convinced that this it is not because of any lack of goodwill from all those professionals who have a role in the learning journeys that our young people undertake. We all want the best for them, and we all want to play a part in helping them to achieve their best.

That said, we don't always agree on what we need to do to optimise their chances of future success. We may do too little for them – or far too much. We may try to get ahead of them – or we may try to pull them back. Whatever we do, we can't just rely on our good intentions to turn into practical action, and nor can they.

This book is a way to turn our good intentions into smart and sensible actions. It can help anyone who is interested in improving the life chances of our young people by providing insights into what they need to learn in order to live well and to earn well, and how we can help them do so.

The futures of young people are challenging and exciting. But there are no blueprints for how they will live in the future. Work is no longer separate from school or from home. Living is no longer separate from learning. Play is no longer just for children. Communities and markets are no longer just local. Production and consumption are no longer separate activities. It is time, therefore, to find some way of speaking across our boundaries when we want to, to share a common language about how we might do things better – and what we should stop doing.

As an educator, I know how much time good teachers need to spend – and do spend – on our professional learning. What we read usually comes from professional associations, recent research and our colleagues, as well as from employers wanting to engage us in systemic reform or organisational restructure.

As an employer of young people in a research institute, I know that good employers are constantly on the look-out for the latest information they can get on how best to acquire and maintain the workforce skills that are relevant to their business futures. We spend as much time as we can afford updating ourselves about labour market realities, policy reform, new training programs, new ways of assessing and evaluating workforce skills, and so on.

As a parent in a blended family, I know that good parenting is a much more complex issue in contemporary times, and that many of us spend a great deal of our time engaging with literature – self-help books, seminar materials, professional advice – to ensure that we do the best we can for our children. This can, of course, increase our anxiety as well as building our parenting expertise.

As a member of policy-making bodies, I know that it is a struggle to achieve a one-size-fits-all framework that is informed by the latest research and is sensitive to the winds of opinion constantly blowing across the public landscape – including the sensitivities of journalists and politicians. It's a 'two steps forward and one step back' process that usually ends up in compromise, and it can be a slow and difficult process.

What all this means is that good educators, employers, parents and policy-makers all need to be well informed, but we rarely read from the same sources. We are all stakeholders in the futures of young people, yet we go to very different places to find out what is best for them. This is not a bad thing – we are, after all, making different con-tributions to their lives. But it does mean that, if and when we come together as common stakeholders in the futures of young people, we struggle to communicate with each other, despite the fact we all share the same wish that they be well prepared for the challenges they will face 'over the horizon'. We tend to speak in dialects, and we leave it to young people to make sense of it all. We rely on them to make the connections, even if we can't do so ourselves. This means that shared goals keep falling down the cracks between us.

The strategy I have adopted in this book is to work across these cracks. In the words used by Ronald Burt, cited in chapter 7, I have tried to fill the 'structural holes' that divide us – the holes that stop us from seeing beyond our own role in preparing young people for a very complex and uncertain future. Because of the importance of plugging the holes, I have tried to use as little jargon as possible. If and when I use it, I hope that I have provided enough clues or explanations to allow anyone to access the key ideas in each chapter.

No special knowledge is needed to read the book. However, this does not mean that every idea in the book is a simple one. The future is so complex that it makes no sense to rely solely on tips and techniques. In fact, I do make some strong criticisms of this approach in chapter 3, when speaking of taking shortcuts to building creative capacity. The book follows a 'jigsaw' path, with each chapter opening up one key theme relevant to the preparation of young people for creative futures.

Chapter 1 explains what creativity is and why it is so important to young people's working lives. It shows how 'second-generation' thinking about creativity opens it up to everyone, not just a few geniuses. Chapter 2 explores the identity of 21st-century young people – what I call the 'Yuk/Wow' Generation. Chapter 3 looks at our current education systems, explaining their importance and their irrelevance to creative futures. Chapter 4 outlines changes to the industrial culture of the workplace and the implications of this for employers and employees. Chapter 5 takes up the challenge of teaching differently, while chapter 6 takes up a similar theme in relation to the challenge of becoming a self-managing and autonomous learner rather than merely a passive and complaint one. Chapter 7 provides a vision of what a creative self-managing learner might become, and how we can build learning environments in educational, home and work settings that enable 'high-flying'. Chapter 8 takes up the thorny question of how to assess or evaluate creative capacity, insisting that we do need to assess it, and we need to do so in authentic and credible ways. Finally, chapter 9 looks at what we have said before, and are saying now, about the future and the implications for young people joining the workforce.

My interest is in young people from early years to doctoral studies and how to educate them better in the broadest sense of the word. I am neither an economist, a labour market analyst, a social futurist, nor a cognitive psychologist, although I do draw on all these fields to understand what sort of learning young people need in the 21st century and how it differs from previous centuries. I am also unapologetically focused on youth, despite the fact that the potential to work as 'creatives' is not owned by young people alone.

While I have written the book for a global audience, many of the examples, data samples and examples are taken from Australian sources. This is not just because it is more convenient to do so; it is also because Australia is the national context with which I am most familiar. I feel that this familiarly allows me to make more confident claims about how the specifics of certain practices work as exemplars of wider global trends.

I do provide examples of good practice, but I don't pull these neatly together in order to give stakeholders a formula for taking instant action. To do so would be contrary to the assumptions I make about the task: that collapsing the complexity of creative capacity is as unhelpful as insisting on its mystery. Instead, I map what is going on and why we need to pay attention to new cultural forms and developments, and what all this means for how we work with young people on a daily basis. We must offer something better, not just more of the same. This book is a guide for doing just that.

Creativity is everyone's business

More than a century ago, Charles Darwin saw a wood-pecking finch in the Galapagos Islands feeding on insects found within tree bark. It did not have a beak long enough or hard enough to extract them. So it used a cactus thorn, held in its beak. This allowed the finch to behave as if it were a woodpecker. At some time in the past, the first 'carpenter' finch must have selected the first twig or cactus spine that did the job and begun to carry it around. Now all carpenter finches on the Galapagos Islands have these skills.

About seventy-five years ago, British blue tits were first observed pecking at the foil tops of milk bottles to feed on the cream underneath. This observation may have been made soon after the first bird worked out how to peck through the first milk bottle cap. Soon all the birds of that species could peck through foil bottle tops and continued to do so well into the next two decades.

Half a century ago, an IKEA employee, Gillis Lundgren, found himself with a problem: how to fit a table in the boot of his car without causing damage to the table legs. He solved the problem by breaking off the legs of the table, then reassembling the entire piece of furniture once he got home. This, IKEA claims, is the 'lucky inspiration' that gave rise to flat packaging.

A decade later, the IKEA store in Stockholm was unable to cope with the massive crowd who flooded in when it first opened. Frustrated customers began to grab items off the storage shelves without waiting for customer service. The subsequent emergence of the do-it-your-self (DIY) customer culture, IKEA claims, originated with this service 'inadequacy'.

The above four stories have a lot in common. If we accept Arthur Koestler's long-standing definition of creativity as the 'defeat of habit by originality', then these stories are all about creativity in action. The capacity to use tools had not been in the behavioural repertoire of finches – until it happened. The capacity to peck open milk bottle tops was not in the behavioural repertoire of blue tits – until it happened. Cutting the legs off tables that don't fit into the family sedan was not habitual practice for furniture-makers; nor was letting customers enter the storeroom behind the counter to help themselves. In each case, habitual practice was overturned by taking an original approach to a problem and thereby turning the problem into an opportunity. In the case of IKEA, some person or persons were imaginative enough to think of a minus as a plus. And this, in the long run, was the start of something big and beneficial for IKEA and its growing cohort of customers.

There is a postscript to the formula that is a legacy of the IKEA stories; that is, IKEA + creativity = business success. IKEA's DIY culture means that all of us who enter an IKEA store and leave with a flat pack-age have further activity to become engaged in. If you are not like me, you will have succeeded in assembling the object you wanted exactly as you saw it in the store and on the package. If you are like me, you will have become frustrated by your inability to get to this point without making quite a few errors on the way. In this sense IKEA has made a problem for more than a few of us. They are asking us to become expert assemblers of household furniture whether or not we have the skills or the desire to do so. The low price tag is a great incentive.

Like the problem that became an opportunity in each of the stories above, this problem (that is, how to follow the written instructions that come in the IKEA flat pack) is also an opportunity. It is no accident that the Chinese character for 'problem' or 'crisis' is also the character for 'opportunity'. The frustration of trying to follow 'how to assemble' instructions provide many comedians with great comic material. At the time of writing, YouTube has on its website an amusing commercial that does a neat job of lampooning IKEA instructions. In similar vein, the Australian Broadcasting Commission's TV program, *The Chaser's War on Everything*, has targeted IKEA's 'post-production' as more than worthy of parody. The result? More creativity (script-writing, editing, co-authorship, serious play) leading to innovation (ideas that are made into tangible marketable products and processes (TV shows, brands, commercial success), leading to greater productivity (cash, comedy, collaboration).

So what is creativity?

There is no neat answer to the question 'What is creativity?', but we certainly know a lot more about it than we once did. You need only to go into your local bookshop to see how many versions of creativity are competing for space in the 'creativity' market. In a review of academic literature, academic Richard Greene found more than 500 articles on creativity written since 1996. He concludes that the field of creativity is full of concepts 'so attenuated, extenuated, or misunderstood that operationalising of the key concepts is missing or impossible'.[1] He tried to bring some order to this field, designing a meta-model of 42 models of creativity, consisting of 7 types of models, with 6 models in each type, and 13 types of 303 variables. This takes a lot of effort, but unfortunately it does not bring us much closer to understanding what creativity is, except that it is a hot topic and hotly contested.

At a conference I attended on the theme of creativity in higher education, I saw evidence of this excitement and contestation, as the various speakers pushed and pulled creativity like the Pope's robes to cover their priority knowledge object: social justice, transdisciplinarity, learning styles, urban savvy, digital literacy, individual talent and so on. Creativity can begin to collapse under the weight of so many expectations and advocacies. But it can also take root and flourish.

Creativity becomes democratic

Amid all this confusion, there is a newly emerging picture of creativity that explains why there is so much fuss about it. Simply put, we are seeing a shift from what I have called first-generation creativity – also called 'big C' creativity.[2] We have seen a declining interest in the type of creativity that Paul Johnson, in his book *Creators: From Chaucer to Walt Disney*, characterises as 'a painful and often terrifying experience to be endured rather than relished and preferable only to not being a creator at all'.[3] In its place, we have seen the rise of a new wave of 'little c' literature (second-generation thinking[4]) that focuses typically on the thinking and doing of a much greater proportion of the population than a few towering historical figures who have huge IQs and 'the most ferocious self-discipline'.[5] Robert Weisberg's *Creativity* (2006),[6] Jonathon Feinstein's *Nature of Creative Development* (2006), and *Creativity and Development*, a 2003 round table discussion of experts in the field, are typical of this democratising turn. This shift to a more open and inclusive notion of creativity is summarised in table 1.1 (p. 10).[7]

In second-generation creativity, self-discipline – although perhaps not so demanding as to be termed 'ferocious' – has a key role to play in thinking and doing. What the creative turn is precisely not about is amplifying the myth that creativity is a light bulb that is more likely to go off in the head of a genius once all restraint is removed, including self-restraint. The necessary self-discipline for creativity is not about Puritan self-abnegation. It does not require the 'user' to deny instant gratification, although it may sometimes be needed to stay in the grey of unresolvability rather than rushing to task completion. The disciplined self-management needed for second-generation creativity to flourish comes from understanding the conditions in which one can work optimally with others, based on self-knowledge about how best to contribute to a shared project or organisational goal. This sort

Table 1.1

A comparison of first-generation and second-generation creativity

First-generation creativity concepts	Second-generation creativity concepts
Serendipitous, non-economic	'Hard' and an economic driver
Singular – belongs to individuals	Pluralised/team-based
Spontaneous – arising from the inner self	Dispositional and environmental
Outside the box or any other metric	Requires rules and boundaries
Arts-based	Transdisciplinary – found across all subject areas
Natural or innate	Learnable
Not amenable to teaching	Teachable
Not assessable	Assessable

of self-knowledge makes it possible for individuals to discern 'good inhibitors' from those things that merely constrain them and to understand the conditions in which apparent obstacles can be enablers. The big shift is from control and command from without to assessment and management from within. Just as importantly, it is about a disposition to connectivity rather than to individual egotism.

It is worth noting that the democratic turn in the literature parallels a democratic turn more generally in our social lives – in designing, editing and in content creation. Every time we use a drop-down menu and select a preferred font – will it be Times New Roman or Courier? – we make a design decision. Tools such as PowerPoint, Word, digital cameras, Photoshop and so on make it possible for us to select, cut and paste what we want and how we want it. This means that more of us are confidently bringing a DIY disposition to aesthetic tasks rather than leaving it all to the experts. In doing so we share the pleasures (and some of the frustrations) of the creative designer.

The creative workforce

This does not mean the death of specialisms or technical expertise. We still need to use disciplinary knowledge and to understand how to make complex software work for us. But it does mean that we are more likely to anticipate working in partnership with experts than previous generations, and more likely to have 'done our homework' before, during and after negotiations with experts. The popularity of house renovation in Australia may not be explicable only in social researcher Hugh Mackay's terms – as a retreat from large-scale political and environmental issues – but in terms of the affordances (that is, the tools and networks we now have) to make aesthetic as well as functional decisions about our personal built environment. As is true of the creative class in general, design decisions are not just merely the province of interior decorators and other similar middle-class professions. They are available to young and old, rich and poor alike.

It doesn't take a genius

So creativity is not the same as 'giftedness'. In former educational times, the word 'gifted' was an exclusive category reserved for a high IQ or artistic elite. Later, the category was stretched by special educators and social psychologists to become an inclusive category, the proposition that we are all gifted in different ways being much more palatable for a democratic schooling ethos.

But there is danger in following the trend from exclusivity to inclusivity. If we move too quickly to the proposition that 'everyone is creative, really' just as we decided that 'everyone is gifted, really', then creative capacity can remain undifferentiated from our broad humanity and becomes a target for formulaic developmental packages. Once formularised as development knowledge, it is more likely to appear in the idiom of economics, technology and management. This renders it vulnerable to theoretical models that offer the most generalisability or appear to offer the greatest predictability or semblance of control over behaviour and events.[8] The 'Ten Quick Steps to a More Creative You', while perhaps inevitable as the next volume in the dizzying number of self-help publications that promise instant, ego-enhancing identity transformation, is unlikely to signal a conceptual breakthrough in creative capacity-building. In simple terms, 'dumbing down' creativity is not a shortcut to fostering it.

Figure 1.1 is one example of this sort of creativity 'packaging', coming as an unsolicited email to the author's desk.[9]

A number of features of this workshop advertisement are characteristic of first-generation thinking. The first is that 'creativity' and 'genius' are taken as inextricably linked. One couldn't imagine being creative without being or becoming a genius. Second, creativity-as-genius is all about individual cognitive power. It comes from comes from inside an individual's head and is 'unleashed' if and when that individual learns the correct brain techniques. The requisite 'tips and techniques' are available through the workshop, and they 'will have you churning out sensational ideas in no time'. Ideas – and some ready cash.

What this framing of creativity does is to disconnect creativity-as-genius from a particular context or experience, making it into a go-anywhere, do-anything tool that can be built into the brain during a one-off, 9-to-5 seminar. And once you have the formula, the secret, the knack, there will be no stopping you. So contextual issues such organisational culture and climate, or learning dispositions such as a propensity for risk-taking, tolerance of ambiguity and openness to critique, are relegated to the fringes of creative capacity-building. Individual cognition is all.

The research evidence provided to support the claims made about the dramatic decline in an individual's creative abilities over time is as startling as it is unsupported by evidence. The (unwarranted) claim that 'everyone is creative' but that we lose this power with astonishing speed as we age ensures that every individual not only sees themselves in the picture of creative genius but also sees themselves in danger of having this ability 'run out', just like our planet's fossil fuels, unless they do something about it.

It is not as though many of the skills and abilities named as outcomes of the workshop are not worth having. The problem is that developmental knowledge about creative capacity is rendered individual, exclusively brain-centred and formulaic, applying 'to everywhere

The creative workforce

Figure 1.1
Email advertisement for creativity enhancing workshop

Here's how to unleash your Creative Genius!

Imagine what one or more brilliant ideas could do to improve your career success!

Have you ever wanted to come up with winning original ideas? ... Does your job demand that you develop new ideas and fresh approaches? ... Do you ever want to break the mould and be the 'thought leader'? ... Do you need more ideas more often?

What about these creative challenges ...

↪ Trying to engage others in the creative process ...

↪ Moving from a good idea to a well-delivered outcome ...

↪ Finding people to share your ideas and excitement with ...

↪ Building a brains trust to help with the development and refine your ideas ...

If you can relate to any of these then I have some good news for you. Let me explain ...

Everyone is creative! However, often this creativity is buried under years of non-creative conditioning and linear work practice. In fact research has proven that non-creative behaviour is learned. Here's what happens to our creative ability over time ...

↪ At 5 years of age, 90% are creative

↪ At 12 years of age, 30% are creative

↪ At 17 years of age, 10% are creative

↪ At 30+ years of age, 2% are creative

The *Creative Impact*™ workshop has been specifically designed to allow you to see that you can be fantastically creative. It will arm you with loads of tools, techniques, know-how and insight so you can unleash your natural creative genius.

and nowhere, everybody and nobody'.[10] 'You too can be a genius, and in only 8 hours' is not a strategy for building tomorrow's creatives. A better start would be to have young people learn how to spot shonky evidence and unsubstantiated claims.

The sort of advocacy for creative capacity exemplified above gives creativity a bad name among all reasonably well-educated and thoughtful people. Unfortunately, this can often mean that they back away from any attempt to define or 'capture' creativity. It seems more reasonable to see it as so mysterious and serendipitous that it defies definition. Thus it also defies any attempt to foster it systematically. Moreover, it is still widely held that creativity is relevant to only a small percentage of graduates as future professional workers. So it can be and has been pretty much ignored in the halls of academe, its relevance limited to achievements in artistry, not industry. Artistry is still perceived as opposed to science, as 'soft' as opposed to 'hard'. Thus creativity's potential contribution to 21st-century problem-solving (for example to issues of environmental sustainability, poverty eradication and social betterment) remains unacknowledged in most universities, despite rhetorical flourishes that speak of formal education's invaluable contribution to a more informed, equitable and productive society.

Creativity is for everyone

Second-generation creativity is everyone's business. It is not a capacity that is limited to comedy writers or business organisations or indeed to the assemblers of IKEA furniture. Yet this has been a very difficult message to sell about creativity. Perhaps it is because we have used the word 'creative' to talk about 'fudging' results ('creative' accounting covers a multitude of management sins!). Or perhaps too many of us have been exposed as children to 'creative' puzzles designed to keep us busy (and deeply frustrated) for hours. As Dylan Thomas cryptically put it, 'Oh, easy for Leonardo!'

Then again, we may have run the gauntlet of drama class experiences designed to make us as 'creative' as those happy few who come to love the roar of the greasepaint and the smell of the crowd. In the stage-show *A Chorus Line*, one of the dancers reminisces, unhappily, about being enrolled in a drama class in which she is told to 'feel the cold and the snow and the air' while pretending to ski. She desperately tries to feel all the things her classmates say they feel, but she admits to feeling precisely nothing. Whether we can stare at a blurred sketch and see a cow, or whether we can 'feel' something that is not real to us, is not a measure of creativity that is of interest in terms of an authentic workforce future. It is not helpful to collapse 'being creative' into whether we can act, sing, dance or do cryptic puzzles.

My own experience of this syndrome has brought home to me how deeply disquieting it is to be the only one in the room who cannot see the cow, or who cannot think of fifty-six things to do with a chair, apart from sitting on it. I have certainly learned to marvel at what some people can make of an inkblot or a set of blurred shapes and, like most young children, I did lie on my back as a five-year-old imagining that clouds were everything from sailing ships to sausages. But I do not feel that we need to be condemned to seeing creativity as 'out of the box' imagining of this sort.

A third possibility exists: that creativity has been too whimsical an idea for us to get our collective head around. Unfortunately, as learning theorist and educational reformer Guy Claxton sees it, the most pervasive understanding of creativity in our culture is that it is 'a rare and exotic mental ability that stands apart from normal cognition'.[11] It is not a matter of putting flesh on the bones – for most people there are no bones! Creativity remains mysterious and unknowable, a ghostly spirit living in a light bulb that appears spontaneously and without warning over someone's inspired head.

My own research into how university academics understand creativity bears this out.[12] A significant number of my colleagues in the higher education sector see creativity as something that is possessed by individuals who have a natural gift for thinking 'outside the square', and think that it flourishes only when rules are removed. As a colleague of mine declared recently, 'The only thing you can do is get out of their way!' This sort of thinking disqualifies any of us from bringing much to bear on building creative capacity. We need only sit back and watch – a comforting thought for those who want an easy life because it leaves all the work to one individual's 'creative genius'.

There are many more 'creatives' than Mozart

The good news is that we are not condemned to thinking of creativity in any of these de-limited ways. While we would always hope to see future Mozarts, Matisses and Michelangelos, and while we know that we are most unlikely to be able to 'prepare' such individuals, they are not the beginning and end of the creativity story. Nor do they constitute the bulk of those whom Richard Florida, in his book *Rise of the Creative Class*, calls 'creatives'.[13]

Florida's 'creatives' can tell us much about the dispositions and *modus operandi* of creative workers of the future. They are not solitary individuals of artistic genius. Nor are they reducible to a collective of computer nerds, although technology and its affordances play a significant role in shaping their professional and social interests. They are people from all socioeconomic and ethnic backgrounds who can utilise their skills in a much broader terrain of commercial settings than the entertainment and 'lifestyle' industries. They are closely connected to their informational and relational networks, and are likely to be found working in such fields as business, finance, law, education and health care, not just in computer graphics and the digital and creative industries alone.

Richard Florida makes it clear that 'coolness' – of lifestyle, friends and location – is a hallmark of the 'creative class'. He provides an example of a young, oddly coiffed Texan with high-tech skills who chooses to live in Austin, because of its 'thriving music scene, ethnic and cultural diversity, fabulous outdoor recreation and great nightlife', rather than Pittsburgh with its good job prospects but lack of cultural colour and movement.[14] Florida sees this disposition as no longer 'alternative' but the new 21st-century creative mainstream:

> This young man and his lifestyle proclivities represent a profound new force in the economy and life of America. He is a member of what I call the creative class: a fast-growing, highly educated, and well-paid segment of the workforce on whose efforts corporate profits and economic growth increasingly depend. Members of the creative class do a wide variety of work in a wide variety of industries – from technology to entertainment, journalism to finance, high-end manufacturing to the arts. They do not consciously think of themselves as a class. Yet they share a common ethos that values creativity, individuality, difference, and merit.[15]

For Florida, a prosperous economic future depends not just on the ability to attract 'creatives' like this high-tech Texan but also to translate the economic advantage their exceptional combination of skills bring in the form of new ideas, new high-tech businesses and regional growth. He is blunt and unequivocal about this fact: 'Places that succeed in attracting and retaining creative class people prosper; those that fail don't.'[16]

Florida's analysis of the creative class is not universally applauded. Like many thinkers who throw a metaphorical hand grenade into an orderly field, he has many critics, who accuse him of making misleading or exaggerated claims and thereby breeding sensationalism rather than more real explanatory power. He has been accused of over-blowing the centrality, size and significance of the creative class and the related significance of urban amenities and their consumption.[17] Accusations that he is too yuppie-focused, too classist and populist, too ready to quantify qualitative difference, and too quick to make links between the gay culture and technology, have come thick and fast. One critic sums up her objections this way: 'What he is selling is not the virtues of creativity but the ingredients of a formula.'[18]

All this ferment has been good for thinking about the link between creativity and the workforce, attesting as it does to the power of Florida's ideas to reach a wide and eclectic audience. For some his populism is exciting; for others it is tedious and self-promoting. While we do not have to say an unqualified 'yea' or 'nay' to Florida's gospel, few could doubt that his analysis offers much – because of its controversy as much as because of its analytic – to our thinking about the relationship between economic, social and workforce futures of young people, including those who have been marginalised in Western economic systems. In other words, the Florida 'industry' is proving to be a very productive one.

So what more do we know about how 'creatives' engage with their social world? We do know that they prefer a workplace environment that is flexible and not restrictive in terms of dress codes or hours. In Florida's terms, they mirror the lifestyles of a previous generation of artists, musicians and academics who 'can never be forced to work yet were never truly not at work'.[19] They are, like their bohemian predecessors, less likely to be driven by dollars than by the challenge of the work they might be able to do and the lifestyle they want to enjoy. This does not mean that their motives are benevolent or altruistic. It means that they are unlikely to be lured into staying in a dull or tedious workplace by the offer of an incremental salary increase alone. They are more likely to opt for a peripatetic lifestyle, prepared to move early and often if and when the opportunity presents itself.[20]

What sets this group apart from other 'professions' or 'classes', however, is not any sense of social coherence – they are as disparate and heterogeneous as the mavericks of the past. They are different because what they produce and the sort of industry in which they are productive are no longer at the edge of big business. They have shifted from the margins of economic and social life to its core.

Creativity demands real effort

While they may prefer 'collarless' and flexible work environments, Florida's creatives are neither shiftless nor unreliable when it comes to productivity. They add value to an organisation or enterprise by engaging in high-level problem-solving that is possible only through a strong combination of intellectual power, interactivity and capable judgment. They work hard because the problems they wrestle with are tough nuts to crack. They are not solved by routine thinking or by following simple templates.

This means that 'creatives' need to be well educated in and beyond the foundational disciplines, because they utilise high levels of literacy and numeracy in order to work across the domains of the conceptual and the aesthetic. This allows them to produce something different and useful by way of networked communication, big picture translation and repurposing information by viewing linkages across disparate fields of knowledge and activity.

The value of these creative workers lies in their capacity to adapt or recombine ideas for novel purposes, rather than inventing something out of nothing. Once again, this flies in the face of the 'genius' myth. Take a bookshop, take a coffee shop. What can be made at the intersection of both so that something new becomes possible? For Mary Ryan Bookshops, the answer is a hybrid space in which both functions are combined into a comfortable, almost intimate lifestyle space, a living room rather than two shops.

As a less obvious example, let's take dogs and wine. What can and has been made at the intersection of these is a book about dogs whose owners run wineries. The book *Wine Dogs: The Dogs of Australasian Wineries* has been so popular that it has been reprinted in a glossy version for its robust market.[21]

As Thomas Watson Jr, founder of computer giant IBM, put it, 'Good design is good business.' It follows that what is good for business will be much in demand as a set of skills, attributes or dispositions in the professional worker. According to Richard Florida, nearly a third of our workforce will need or have acquired such skills by 2015. Moreover, they will not just be those who can afford 'high-end' private schooling or those who are the highest achievers in traditional school exams, although they will need to be good learners. Nor will they necessarily be the 'cool' or 'alternative' kids who are into rap, truancy and body piercing. They can and will come from any demographic and any location.

Wherever they come from, they will have a capacity to generate their output at high speed. This speeding up of workplace productivity is an effect of the dramatic reduction in the duration of the full product cycle. Relationship marketing, global competition, boom and bust cycles, and rapid technological change have all seen the product cycle of Innovation-to-Diffusion-to-Stasis accelerate from the 1970s (when the Innovation period could range from six to thirty-two years and the Diffusion period fifteen to twenty years) to become, in 2000, a cycle of one to five years for Innovation and one to five years for the Diffusion phase to be completed. Indeed, the digital company Intel has found that 90 per cent of the products it delivers on the last day of the calendar year did not exist on the first day of that same year.[22] The pace of technological change and social invention has likewise seen an astonishing reduction in time taken to communicate with 50 million people worldwide: from thirty years (radio), to thirteen years (television), to less than four years (World Wide Web).

The ratcheting-up of processes of production and distribution means that workers who can create and disseminate products fast, and can work at more than one phase of the cycle, are more valuable than those whose skills are delimited by an old industrial model of one small link in a slow-moving supply and demand chain. Indeed, the idea of 21st-century workers as links in a productivity chain is now outmoded. So too is the idea that users and producers – or creators and audiences – need to be thought of as separate categories.

Creativity means that everyone's active

The fundamental shift in the way that value creation is thought about in innovative business organisations is a response to the fact that post-millennial consumption is no longer essentially passive in character. Put another way, the idea of supply as passing through links in a chain to a 'sit and get' customer is increasingly irrelevant. Customers and producers are all actively engaged as co-creators of value in a value-adding network, not a chain. After a generation or more of 'couch potato' inactivity at the end of a supply chain, whereby what is to be consumed arrives as a final product, we are now seeing patterns of distribution and consumption being developed that allow everyone in the production network to add value to the product.

This shift in consumer–supplier relations has brought with it a change in the configuration of supply itself. A supply or value chain, according to public policy analyst Greg Hearn, 'is a simple, one-way, linear process', with value creation essentially being limited to 'reducing transaction or distribution costs'.[23] The shift to a value network is consumer-centric rather than linear. It 'involves processes of reiteration and feedback' in which 'movement may occur from any one point to any other point' with 'horizontal links cutting across institutional boundaries to put people in direct contact with each other'.[24] Creative workers move quickly within and across these networks, bypassing nodes that have ceased to add value, just as water flows around rocks. Where nodes of exchange do not add value, they can – and will – be bypassed.

At a recent celebration of twenty or so highly successful alumni of my university, it became evident to all of us present that these out-standing professionals had more than one thing in common. Apart from being outstandingly successful once they had graduated from the institution, all of them were border-crossers. All of them had moved – indeed, leapt – from one disciplinary or professional context into another with confidence and agility. Many seemed poised to do so again. Their fundamental curiosity about a world yet to be explored, their capacity to tolerate temporary discomfort in the interests of personal and professional growth, their determination to move on just when they might have settled down to a predictable work pattern, and their success in adding value to their respective work organisation – all of these qualities, dispositions and achievements were palpable in the stories they told about themselves and their life trajectories.

A few of these outstanding alumni thanked their teachers. Others made little or no mention of the contribution of their experience of formal learning to the way they engaged with other people in other places. In many cases, the audience was left to guess at what precisely their education had contributed to their high-flying professional capacities. Formal education may, in fact, have had little to do with the creative capacity and life trajectory so evident in these individuals, whether or not they thanked their teachers. Put bluntly, the value that formal learning adds to the 'boundary-less' careers of creative professionals, and how we might move deliberately to foster such attributes through our schools and universities, were either mysterious or missing at that celebration.

This fact made me reflect on whether or not we might be able to capture and extract some of the positives that were embedded in the learning environments and social relationships that these high-flyers had experienced. Was it just happenstance – the luck of having a really effective teacher or mentor? Was it the company they kept and how they moved in and out of new social relationships that allowed them to learn and incorporate new capacities into their repertoire of skills? How did they know when to move and when to stay? Was it nature or nurture, or both? And finally, did they fit the profile of Florida's 'creatives' and, if not, did this matter?

It has become evident to me since this event that Florida's 'creatives' are not the only people who need and will benefit from increased creative capacity. According to the *Cox Review of Creativity in Business*, 'Creativity shouldn't be restricted to "creatives", it needs to flow through the entire company.'[25] I realised that, if we are to understand what role formal education can play in preparing the future creative workforce, we need first to dispel the prevailing ideas about creative capacity, even those that Florida has been so successful in promulgating. It is not necessary to measure the size and location of a newly emerging 'creative class' to understand the value of creative capacity-building for all young people, nor is it necessary to measure the economic productivity of the 'creative industries' to understand how much creativity can and will define the life well lived.

The fact that Florida's 'creatives' are closely tied to an enterprise setting does not mean that all creative capacity can or should be dragooned into the service of industry alone. Much of the creative activity that draws on digital tools and technology is done for no other purpose than the pleasure of engagement. It is neither the money nor the fame but the sheer delight of producing something from something else – of cutting and pasting images, sounds, words, some of which are your own while others come from the person next door or on the other side of the world. It is for living, not just earning a living.

To imagine the twenty-first century as an era rich with creative possibilities, we need to let go of the idea that creativity is an attribute of a privileged genetic elite. Creativity does not simply gush forth from some mysterious place within a few select individuals, nor does it do so despite the prevailing social conditions. This means that creativity can be developed through appropriate processes in an appropriate learning environment.

Before we consider what this environment might look like, which I do in the chapters that follow, I want to demolish another myth that can prevent us from seeing how important creativity is to all of us.

Creativity is not just for toddlers

The very breadth of activity that can count as 'creative' is a turn-off for thinking expert Edward de Bono. He says that 'the word "creativity" in English is too broad and ranges from creating a mess to painting a masterpiece'.[26] In calling us to consider the messes that result from creativity, de Bono evokes the early childhood classroom, a place where every effort is made to ensure that little hands have the pleasure of close engagement of the messy and manic kind. Messes are fine – even cute – when hands are tiny.

One of the myths that prevail about creativity is that it is terrific as arts education for toddlers' growth and development but that adults need to do less of it because they have grown and developed into mature social beings. In educational circles, there has long been a strong advocacy of creative expression as the key to optimal social and emotional development.[27] And there is no doubt about the value of aesthetic learning for young children. But this makes for a problem. The fact that creativity is so closely identified with early years arts education makes it difficult to take creativity seriously after primary school. The further we move away from the early years, the more likely it is that creativity (arts education for toddlers) becomes garnish to 'serious' high-stakes subjects like English, maths and science. In most education-speak, the word 'creative' is invariably followed by the word 'arts', with arts being the 'cute and flabby' side of an arts/science binary. If and when it does reappear, it is used as a means to re-engage those kids who are either school drop-outs or at risk of becoming so. Once again, this is laudable, but it also puts creativity on the edge of the main game, not in the centre of it. It collapses it into remedial mess-making – right for risky adolescents but suspect for smart adults.

This myth flies in the face of all the evidence that we have about the lifelong and life-wide value of creativity. Creativity is now being acknowledged as an observable and valuable component of all social and economic enterprise, from cradle to grave. It is not garnish to the productivity roast but fundamental to an increasingly complex, challenge-ridden and rapidly changing economic and social order. In the terms of social psychologist Mihaly Csikszentmihalyi, creativity is 'no longer a luxury for the few, but ... a necessity for all'.[28] Increasingly, economists and policy-makers are embracing creativity, innovation and human talent as essential capacities for economic growth and social dynamism. The burgeoning field of scholarship on creativity is demonstrating the economic importance of digital content industries such as computer games, digital video and film, post-production, animation and websites. Put simply, creativity is not only about masterpieces, mess-making or money-making. It is also a means for living better and learning more.

Creativity is something from something else

Another powerful myth about creativity is that it is about making something from nothing. Being creative rarely means this. Creative capability has much more to do with holding disparate things together long enough to generate a new or third space or idea, or, as Norman Jackson puts it, they 'move an idea from one state to another'.[29] The 'creatives' quoted below all echo this idea:

> 'I'm interested in the moment when two objects collide and generate a third. The third object is where the interesting work is.' (Bruce Mau, designer)

> '[I want] to perceive the relations between thoughts, or things or forms of expression that may seem utterly different and be able to combine them.' (William Plomer, poet)

> 'New discoveries in science and mathematics often consist of the synthesis between theories or concepts which have hitherto been regarded as unconnected.' (Anthony Storr, historian)

> 'You can take two substances, put them together and produce something powerfully different (table salt), sometimes even explosive (nitroglycerine).' (Diane Ackerman, writer)[30]

In the same spirit as those quoted above, Albert Einstein once explained creativity as a form of combinatorial play that connected concepts rarely combined. This demands an ability to hold a large number of associations together in the mind, then select the particular associations that offer interesting possibilities. As explained by psychologist Teresa Amabile and her colleagues: 'It's as if the mind is throwing a bunch of balls into the cognitive space, juggling them around until they collide in interesting ways. The process has a certain playful quality to it … If associations are made between concepts that are rarely combined – that is, if the balls that don't normally come near each other collide – the ultimate novelty of the situation will be greater.'[31] Once 'ultimate novelty' is there for all to see, it is often mistaken for the outpouring of the pure and unadulterated genius of one individual when it is in fact the outcome of a number of persons, activities and disciplined deliberations, including the rejection of many alternative combinations.

This as true of artistic performance as it is of scientific and technological 'breakthroughs'. Michael Jackson's famous moonwalk is a good example. According to one of his biographers, J. Randy Taraborrelli, the 'genius' was not that Jackson 'invented' it but that he knew what to combine and how, drawing on performances (and discarded ideas) from the past and present:

> Michael hadn't invented any of these moves; the poses were modified versions of 'locking', a street dance form of the 1970s. The moonwalk was a move TV's Soul Train dancers had discarded almost three years earlier. Sammy Davis, Jr, James Brown and Jackie Wilson all used to execute that same spin, and going up on the toes is a touch Michael saw Fred Astaire use in his classic films of the 1930s. To combine all those moves, from all those eras – to take different styles and to make them his own – that's Michael's genius as a dancer and creator.[32]

So the capacity to appropriate the ideas of others takes nothing away from the exceptional talent of someone like Michael Jackson. It does not 'expose' such individuals as lesser than they are perceived to be because they derive and combine the ideas and behaviour of other individuals or groups. On the contrary, such individuals deserve recognition for their unique and exciting creative products.

They also deserve recognition for their sheer hard work. Original combinations of ideas, conversations, dance steps, musical scores and artefacts that make original contributions to any realm of human activity are not things that can be bought at the shop. They are hard-won, requiring from their designers a capacity both to reject a prototype acclaimed by others and to endorse a prototype rejected by others. How to make such judgments without being caught on the brambles of self-congratulation or self-condemnation is demanding in what it asks of creatives from one unique moment to next. So creatives are never 'off the hook' of potential failure as well as possibility.

As their own toughest critics, creatives have a disposition to new knowledge that is unrelentingly curious, so much so that, at James Madison University for Assessment and Research, a team of educational psychologists have devised a 'Curiosity Index' of sixteen self-reported items to measure students' capacity for creative engagement through assessing the breadth and depth of students' interest in and engagement with the world around them.[33] They are therefore not easily convinced by simple formulae and spin.

Stephen Bowkett, author of *100 Ideas for Teaching Creatively*, argues that creativity may mark a fifth 'phase of life' category beyond Somatic, Mythic, Romantic and Philosophical: an Ironic phase of examining, questioning, doubting and reconstructing frameworks in a spirit of curiosity, playfulness and experience.[34] This sort of creativity is also the marker of the ironist, someone who enjoys demonstrating that both and neither of two apparently contrary propositions are necessary and true.

Irony is not everyone's cup of tea. As American philosopher Richard Rorty points out, the refusal to provide a final vocabulary of explanation – to tidy up, to praise, condemn or redeem – is likely to be unwelcome in a society that is much more comfortable with advocacy than with ambivalence.[35] However, the refusal to 'reach a conclusion', while frustrating to many, is the very strength of irony, because irony is about 'contradictions that do not resolve into larger wholes, even dialectically, about the tension of holding incompatible things together because both or all are necessary and true'.[36] When we use irony we generate breakthrough ideas by cutting across traditional thinking – in fact, we make it seem strange. Irony doesn't let us 'think straight'. The capacity to make trouble for familiar thinking may be frustrating and annoying to some, but what it offers by way of real

The creative workforce

innovation potential is immeasurable. Irony deficiency, on the other hand, is a squelcher.

The value of irony – of a capacity to work with difference rather than move to resolve it – builds on understandings first made public more than half a century ago by creativity's founding father, Arthur Koestler. In his seminal work *The Act of Creation*,[37] Koestler identified the decisive phase of creativity as the capacity to 'perceive … a situation or event in two habitually incompatible associative contexts'. Following Koestler, the capacity to select, reshuffle, combine or synthesise already existing facts, ideas, faculties and skills in original ways may be understood to be evidence of creativity at work.

David Perkins makes a similar point. In *The Mind's Best Work*, he insists that skills like pattern recognition, creation of analogies and mental models, the ability to cross domains, exploration of alternatives, knowledge of schema for problem-solving, and fluency of thought are indicators of creativity as a set of learning dispositions or cognitive habits.[38] All of this requires a risk-taking disposition, not a disposition to compliance. This is because crossing domains and the exploration of alternatives demand not only agility but also the capacity to tolerate error and not equate it with failure. A risk-taking disposition allows us to learn from the instructive complications of error rather than to hunker down or retreat into compliance and conformity for safety's sake.

To transcend the barriers of habitual thinking, an individual does not have to be a genius, but it does demand a nimble or agile disposition to information processing. It is not about being able to flatten information out quickly in order to provide a simple story or explanation. It is about exercising a gymnastic capacity to work against the grain of sense-making. In the same way that a hurdler has to be agile enough to blur running and jumping, so too creatives are cognitively agile or dextrous enough to thrive in environments where unpredictability and complexity are the norm. Agility is a dynamic ability to create and utilise options at speed and thereby allow organisations to 'gain competitive advantage by intelligently, rapidly and proactively seizing opportunities and reacting to threats'.[39]

Creatives don't linger too long, even in productive spaces. They are suspicious of stasis and/or equilibrium and will dispense with both to jump in the direction of temporary discomfort that might be a potential opportunity. The career of highly successful New Zealand film-maker Peter Jackson is a good example of this. As career analysts Kerr Inkson and Polly Parker point out, his high-profile, project-based, self-managed career demonstrates his capacity not simply to accumulate relevant knowledge but also to move towards dynamism and away from stasis.[40] He did not follow the 'formula' of being close to Hollywood, nor did he rely on formal education to provide him with the relationships and credentials he needed to do his creative work. Instead, he used his career capital – his values and motivation, his career-related skills and expertise, and his social and professional networks – to forge a 'boundary-less' career that made him famous in a highly competitive global industry. His creative output was very much about who he worked with and his judgment about when and how to move to new networks as well as sustaining old ones.

So what?

The nature of creativity remains a much-contested notion. However, second-generation creativity has unhooked the idea of 'being creative' from 'artiness', individual genius and idiosyncrasy, to make it more economically valuable, collaborative, community-based, observable and learnable. It links creativity to an external world of team players, social processes and organisational settings.

This makes it difficult for any of us who are involved in preparing young people for the future to step around creativity's challenge to workforce preparation. It moves us on from the romance of the remote artist-in-a-garret genius who has no need of social engagement, and allows us to focus on ways of thinking and doing that are observable and replicable processes and practices within daily economic and social life. Always and inevitably complex, creativity is now less of a mystery, so it can now be engaged intentionally as an outcome of education. We do not have to wait for the field to be more coherent and self-disciplined to get on with creative capacity-building.

The creative workforce

Creativity involves everyone who is an actively engaged in living, learning and earning in this century. This is because new technology and modes of production make it possible for everyone – indeed they require everyone – to be active co-creators of value for themselves and others, not just passive consumers at the end of a supply-and-demand chain. Processes of production and distribution have accelerated the pace of change and disrupted traditional industrial processes. This makes it unlikely that any of us will be spending long periods in any one place doing only one thing. With so much technological innovation driving new ways of engaging in social activity, our young people are much more likely to be engaged in fast-moving, complex problem-solving than we have been. If our young people can learn to cross borders of all types – disciplinary borders, geographical borders, relational borders –they are more likely to be successful in the world of 21st-century work. They will have the mental and cultural agility to needed to work as 'creatives'.

Young people's capacity to do these things is not just because of – or in spite of – their parents, their schools or their genes. Creativity is not just for a few geniuses, nor is it just for those with a gift for artistic expression. It is the capacity that allows us to be players, not pawns in an increasingly complex world where routines and habits from the past will not serve us well in the future. The good news is that we do not have to wait for nature – or a 'hit or miss' workshop – to provide the moment for creative engagement. While creative capacity may not be able to be directly transmitted or imitated, it is possible – indeed desirable – to teach for the sort of creativity that will be a core capacity for productive 21st-century workers. The chapters that follow explain how this can be done.

The Yuk/Wow Generation

It has been said that kids are alike in many disrespects. For this reason, today's young people are not seen as just the next generation but also as the problem generation. They want it all and want it now. They know too much and too little. They rate style over substance. They don't know what is good for them. And they don't do what they are told.

Of course, this is a perennial story about how young people have been seen by their elders over the centuries. Bemoaning the deficits of the young is a pastime that is as old as Socrates. It is as easy to dismiss these criticisms as it is to endorse them, because we all know at least one kid who is not like this, and we all know many who are. The media makes sure of that. Stories about kids doing outrageous things will sell more advertising space than stories about kids who are community-spirited, outgoing, courteous and considerate.

Our youth have been the focus of more than media attention in the last fifty years. They have been under continuous scrutiny from psychologists and sociologists since the heady days of Marlon Brando as the 'Wild One' and Jimmy Dean as the 'Rebel without a Cause'. Ever since fears of juvenile delinquency – 'the enemy within' – were fuelled by the Cold War moral panics of the 1950s, young people have been probed for any and every symptom of the storm-and-stress of the adolescent 'phase', the stage of development in which they are expected to experience alienation arising from their status confusion and the generation gap.

This is all pretty recognisable to people like me – baby boomers, the first truly 'psychologised' generation. Fifty years later, we still anticipate that many young people will be rude and rebellious in their teen years, but we expect – even hope – that it will pass with the end of adolescence. By the time young people are in their twenties, we generally expect that they will have completed their education, then begin to settle down and become serious about finding a life partner and having a family, a career and a home of their own. As we did – with more or less difficulty!

This familiar script has run its course in the twenty-first century. Things are different now – radically different. Whether we call them Gen Y or Gen Z, the Net Generation, Millennials, Digital Natives, the Online Generation or the Gamer Generation, today's kids are not just the next Problem Generation. Nor are they simply 'going through a phase'. From a very early age, they can choose to live their lives in a profoundly different way from their parents and their siblings – in a parallel universe – even when living under the same roof. They make choices and take chances at unprecedented speed. In a nanosecond they have decided whether something is cool or uncool, whether they want to plug into it or not.

I have chosen to call these young people the Yuk/Wow Generation, because it is a terms that captures the astonishing speed with which young people are likely to make their judgments and the amount of room there is for holding off on judgment-making – none!! I am also using this term because of the problem we have in coming to the end of the alphabet (what happens after Gen Z?) and because it is difficult for many of us to remember when Gen X or Y ends and Z begins. The

Yuk/Wow Generation is simply that generation of young people who will begin to earn their living in the twenty-first century.

Summing up the Yuk/Wow Generation

Here are a few things that neuroscientists, sociologists, psychologists, educators and other experts are saying about the differences between the Yuk/Wow Generation and previous generations.

↳ *Experience rules!* Nothing matters more to the Yuk/Wows than here-and-now experience. They expect constant stimulation, whether in a real-world or a simulated space. They want to be where the action is, somewhere cool with cool people doing cool things. This means that the first question they ask when they answer their mobile phone is more likely to be 'Where are you?' than 'How are you?' The space between a yuk or a wow reaction is a very brief space indeed. They are constantly seeking to find out where the action is and how to get there. Many are parkers, churners and drifters, not long-term committers. They leave choices to the last minute, and they will give priority to lifestyle, self-image and being entertained. They don't see the point of waiting around for years to become qualified or trained, or to save up for what they want, if they can have it now.

↳ *Everything is correctible.* If something doesn't work out, like a university course or a relationship, then Yuk/Wows will move elsewhere. Nothing is forever – anything can be changed and changed quickly. It's a Wikipedia world – Britannica is dead. Success is seen as an outcome of luck as much as thorough planning. As 'gamer' researchers John Beck and Mitchell Wade put it: 'This generation grows up playing games of chance ... They are twice as likely as boomers to believe that success in life is due to luck. This prepares them to shrug off pretty serious setbacks.'[1] For them, anything is possible because there are no agreed values passed down from former generations. It's a patchwork quilt of values and options, and you can make it up – and throw it away – as you go.

→ *Learn it by doing it.* Yuk/Wows prefer to learn by trial and error than to be instructed by their elders. They are impatient with instructions of any sort, because instructions take too long and hold them off from real engagement. They expect to be able to jump over any 'introduction' or preamble and will disengage quickly from anything 'boring', but they can re-engage just as quickly if they think it is seems to be worth it. Their dominant mode of engagement is 'hands on and plugged in', but they also like to work in groups, as long as they are groups that share their interests and their idea of fun. Their preference for multitasking means that they can often give the impression of not paying attention, or at least not paying sufficient attention to what they are being told or shown. They expect parity of esteem in whatever social situation they find themselves, and they are prepared to walk away if they feel that they are not being given sufficient acknowledgment or positive attention.

→ *It's not technology – it's living.* What baby boomers call 'using technology' Yuk/Wows see as simply going about the business of living. They have a different relationship with the electronic world from baby boomers. Technology is not a mystery, and they don't expect e-nirvana – it is so integrated into their lives as to be more like prostheses than gadgets. They are not print-centric – their social engagement is very much focused on the screen, rather than the book. For them, Truth is assembled and dissembled in images and sounds. It comes in the form of endless sound bites, half-baked ideas, gossipy tidbits, all in constant flux. In their world, cut-and-paste is serious play. They like to wear their technology 24/7 – they don't leave it on the desktop. And they also expect it to work 24/7, because that is how they form and maintain so many of their social relationships.

→ *Careers are things that old people have.* Yuk/Wows are unlikely to have a traditional life narrative, and by their mid-teens they already have a different experience of the notion of 'career'. The linear transition from school to work is outmoded – they experience both institutions in parallel. Many Yuk/Wows will have a disrupted pathway to obtaining their formal educational credentials. They are much more likely to experience changes to their study arrangements, including changing or discontinuing courses or combining study and work options. Developmental opportunities (including education) are expected to be just in time, just enough and just down the hall. When shopping for courses, they are buyers of products, not passive consumers of career counsellors' brochures. Non-traditional is the new normal.

↪ *Rebelling is uncool.* While non-traditional is normal, the Yuk/Wows do not seek to make overt collective political statements. Much of their political sensitivity is implicit rather than explicit. Because they are more likely than their parents to have an immigrant grandparent or have a mixed ethnic heritage, their loyalties are not necessarily constructed along traditional Anglo lines of class, ethnicity and gender. This makes them more tolerant of difference in others, but less tolerant of lectures about it from their baby boomer elders. If they don't want to do something, they don't spend time protesting or pleading their case – they simply don't do it. 'Whatever' is their rhetorical shoulder shrug, signalling not so much apathy as the tedium of over-choice and data overload. However, they are alert to sustainability issues, so they approve of having their rubbish recycled – preferably by someone else!

↪ *Nothing is private.* The Yuk/Wows live constantly with surveillance. They have 'helicopter parents' who hover around them almost constantly. They don't expect anything to remain private for long, and they don't share their parents or teachers' concerns about privacy. They don't worry about putting themselves 'out there' on MySpace or You Tube, and they don't particularly worry about stranger danger on the net. However, they know how to subvert surveillance if and when they want to. Texting 'MOS' means 'Mother-over-Shoulder' and PIR 'Parent-in-Room'. They are much less likely to leave the parental home, partly because it would be very expensive to duplicate the lifestyle they enjoy there – they have a separate bedroom, TV, computer and bathroom – and partly because they are allowed to have sex in the parental home, something forbidden to earlier generations. If they do leave home, they are likely to be back early and often – after all, the move is correctible.

↪ *Image matters!* If there is one thing Yuk/Wows can't stand it is being told by their elders not to value style over substance. This is just one of many binaries that has melted as a result of the priority given to the now experience. They have experienced style as a substantive issue in their lives, one that has them replacing their mobile phones with dizzying regularity. They reassess what is 'cool' on a daily or even hourly basis, and this reassessment does not put Style in one column and Substance in another. They know that shopping, cleaning, cooking – that is, maintaining a household – is 'shit' work and they don't want to do it. Having babies is also in the 'too hard' category, at least until their thirties. They don't want jobs that require them to wear 'yuk' uniforms or trades overalls. By and large, they would rather make less money in a 'cool' job – like serving at the juice bar in the town mall – than have a dirty job like plumbing that gives them more cash but no cool.

↪ *Don't trust hierarchies.* While the Yuk/Wows are not overtly political, they do not expect to be treated as low life on a vertical food chain. So they may be the newest kid on the employment block, but they won't be putting their hands up to make the tea or take out the rubbish. In their research into gamers' social attitudes, Beck and Wade found a 'whole generation [who] knows that the "boss" is to be at least ignored, but in many cases, destroyed'.[2] Unlike Moses, they don't respond well to commandments handed down from the mountain top. This can make them appear brash and inappropriately dismissive of rules and regulations, and the people who make them. Yuk/Wows expect to have choices about how, when and where they engage in work, so they expect flexibility from their supervisors. Because they have grown up in small families, they also expect positive personal attention from the adults who feed them, teach them or employ them.

This description is only a brief snapshot of the Yuk/Wow Generation, not an exhaustive treatise. It is possible to see many of the ways in which this generation is similar to other previous generations – at least those who have experienced 'adolescence'. But it is different in two key respects: the speed with which activity options can and do get picked up and dropped, and the massive impact of digital technology in making those choices possible and in giving young people alternatives that previous generations never had.

It needs to be acknowledged again that this description does not apply to all young people at all times and in all places. Nevertheless, it does give us a sense of what they will bring collectively to the workplace of the future. Many of their strengths are also their limitations; in this respect they are no different from any other generation.

Yuk/Wows in the world of work

So how does this snapshot map on to the changing world of work?

First, we need to acknowledge that trends in the social arrangements that pertain to work are just as much a product of the times as trends in youth as a social formation. Both are subject to the same forces – economic, social, technological, political and environmental – that operate at global, national and regional levels, and both also reflect local idiosyncrasies and unique cultural influences.

In broad terms, the shifts and patterns we are seeing in kids' identities and modes of engagement are also being reflected in a diverse array of industries. The trend is towards more technology-enhanced processes, more speedy transactions, more scrutiny of individual, team and organisational performance, more health and safety provisions, more flexibility in dress code, work hours and leave options, and more flattened management structures. Less welcome features in some quarters are the trends towards uncertainty of tenure and less career linearity, particularly in high-tech industries and those that are most exposed to the vicissitudes of global markets.

Not so long ago young people got a full-time paid job and stayed there. Now the picture is 'more like a jigsaw than a straight line', according to Australian social analyst Hugh Mackay.[3] The twenty-first century has relegated permanency of employment to the industrial past. We have seen the decline of full-time work and the rise of part-time, fractional or casual work. This is occurring as the labour market continuously adjusts to the 'off-shoring' of jobs to other global locations, the technologising of many routine jobs and services, corporate downsizing and the feminising of workforce participation.

Australia's robust economy, heavily reliant as it has been on the mining boom, has seen growth in the administrative workforce and in the retail/counter sector (that is, 'face-to-face' work) as well as in full-time employment of more than forty hours per week in managerial, professional and supervisory occupations, most of which are in office and counter work. However, we have also seen a decline in full-time and part-time jobs in the industry sector, and in overall full-time employment of forty hours or less a week. Moreover, the workplace is being perceived in many quarters as a tougher place than in former, less 'calculating' times, with its 24/7 demands, its compressed weeks, its keenly competitive and demanding performance indicators, and its invasion of the home space by information and communication technology.

The decline in overall employment permanency is not a problem for Yuk/Wows, given their propensity as experience-seekers for being 'here today and gone tomorrow'. Nor is 24/7 connectedness a problem – it has been built into their lifestyle well in advance of work. They are comfortable with blurred boundaries between work and home, just as they are comfortable with the idea that 'job security' is a thing of the past.

However, they remain cautious about being straitjacketed by any working arrangements that disallow flexibility and a degree of self-management. As Hugh Mackay puts it, they are a generation 'who seem determined to live life on their own terms, to assert their own values and to keep their options open'. This means that they may seem to be lacking in 'loyalty, commitment or a proper sense of seriousness' in their attitude to work,[4] qualities that would put them on a collision course with many employers, particularly those who seek to maintain a highly regulated, 'top-down' work environment, and are also seeking value for money when it comes investment in on-the-job training.

What is a 'creative' worker identity?

The qualities that might well have Yuk/Wows sparring with traditional workplace managers are, interestingly, the very qualities that give them a head start when it comes to working in the creative economy. According to business strategist John Howkins, the creative economy will be the dominant economic form of the twenty-first century, eclipsing all others not only when it comes to growth in the creation of new products but also in their exploitation, distribution and trade.[5] To be successful in this creative economy, Howkins argues, we will all need a very different set of self-management rules from the ones that have shaped worker identities in the past. They are as follows:

- Invent yourself. Be unique.
- Own your ideas. Put a priority on ideas, not on data.
- Be nomadic. Know when to work alone and when in a group.
- Define yourself by your thinking activities, not your job.
- Learn endlessly. Borrow, reinvent and recycle.
- Exploit fame and celebrity.
- Treat the virtual as real and vice versa.
- Be kind and ambitious, and admire success openly.
- Have fun, and know when to break the rules.[6]

It need hardly be pointed out that these rules do not align with the conformist worker identity we associate with the Western industrial tradition. But they do seem to be remarkably well aligned with many of the attitudes and dispositions of the Yuk/Wow Generation: their high sense of self-regard and self-interest, their focus on what is 'out there' and in putting themselves 'out there', their preparedness to learn by doing rather than following a script, and their capacity to live well in both the real and the virtual worlds.

However, they may struggle when it comes to 'learning endlessly', if they think of learning as memorising and regurgitating information that has been presented by 'knowing' others, or if they think that their formal credentials will provide them with all they need to know, or if they expect to be constantly praised and affirmed for everything they do, or if they feel the need to cling to the safety of familiar things and people.

Today's kids are brave in some respects and timid in others. They have been well nourished, well protected and well treated, so much so that they know little of adversity or what it means to learn from error or failure. They are used to 'soft' landings, and rarely receive the sort of blunt criticism that was once *de rigueur* in the preparation of young people for a public life.

The following are extracts from the Sports Notes section in a private girls' school annual magazine, written seventy years ago. They illustrate the sort of criticisms that young people no longer expect to hear, nor would we expect them to be able to endure them for all posterity, as Miriam, Joyce and Audrey have had to do:

> Miriam ... – Quick in the centre, combines well ... but loses heart.
> Joyce ... – Understands game, but could move a little quicker.
> Audrey ... – Places herself well but lacks height.[7]

The point of this illustration is not that we should return to such overt and public criticism, nor is it to mock the high quality education that this school has been known to give since it was established. The point is that, in our rush to affirm young people in every corner of their lives, we may have left them with little understanding of the value of critical feedback and what can be learned from it. While we have understood that positive parenting and teaching can breed confidence and a sense of self-worth in young people, we have a fair bit of ground to make up when it comes to helping them develop the capacities for tough self-management and self-critique that the highly competitive creative economy demands.

The educational experience has become strange amalgam of some very progressive social attitudes towards young people's rights and some very traditional practices in terms of testing, grading, sorting and credentialling. We 'get tough' in ways that are not very relevant or meaningful in terms of creative capacity-building, and we rush in to massage, stroke and rescue in ways that do not assist young people to learn from the instructive complications of failure. With all that we have learned about learning, we tend to back away from the risks associated with powerful learning when they appear to be at odds with the need to protect young people from negative experiences.

So what?

It is clear that the present generation of young people experiences life very differently in some key respects from past generations. Their ability to interact, engage and disengage, through the affordances of new technology, means that they live by choice, speed and chance. The neat separation of work and non-work is disappearing, along with lifelong careers and secure jobs. This means that the capacities and dispositions needed for work are also changing, and this is reflected in the competitive global labour market.

To work effectively in the fast-moving creative economy, young people will need to acquire a broad and deep array of skills and capacities. Most importantly, they will need a disposition to be active self-managers of their learning, and to exercise authentic self-criticism, if they are to maintain and build the high levels of expertise they will need for the rapidly changing social and technological world. They will also need to build resilience in order to deal with setbacks and delays in achieving their goals.

As educators, employers, parents and policy-makers, we can do better. Indeed, we must do better if the Yuk/Wows are to be well equipped to take their place in the future creative workforce. In the chapters that follow, I have set out an agenda for doing just that.

The creative workforce

'Creative workforce', like 'fun run', sounds like an oxymoron. This is an effect, in part, of our predilection for making a binary out of 'work' and 'play'.

Work, we are taught early and often, is what we are compelled to do to ensure that our most basic needs – food, shelter, security – are met. It is about survival, not creativity. It was what teachers told us to 'get back to' when we were having a good time. It was the tedious and repetitive activity that our parents found for us to do – make our beds, take the rubbish out – before we got to do what we really wanted to do. It is the activity for which many of us expect to receive remuneration, often by way of a fixed salary. It is what we do despite what we would rather be doing.

While many of the world's workers continue to live in a narrowly mechanical, hierarchical world that is a legacy of the Industrial Revolution, most of us want to work in organic organisations as responsible adults. Creativity expert Kevin Byron argues that most workers feel unrewarded for their skills and punished for their failures, citing a recent Gallup poll of 1.7 million employees, which showed that only 20 per cent of workers – or a fifth of the workforce – see themselves as 'having the opportunity to do what they do best every day'.[1]

Play, by contrast, is generally understood to be what we choose to do to relax before or after or despite work. While many of its forms involve keeping to rules – indeed, anything we call 'sport' depends on rules – play invites creative ways of thinking and doing. We don't usually expect extrinsic reward for it in the form of payment or status, but neither do we expect to be punished for it, unless it is illegal, immoral or fattening. In general, and unfortunately, we tend to think of play as something we will do less of as we get older. We will put away childish things in order to 'get serious' about a vocation or career. Play, or 'goofing off', will be relegated to holiday or long service leave, if and when we get it. If we are lucky enough, there may be aspects of our work that allow us to play. But this, we have learnt, will be exceptional. Most of us accept that it is normal to experience working life as 'play-free', filled with demanding and routine ways of thinking and doing rather than with the creative imaginings and fun that we associate with engaging in playful activity.

Work is serious: the Victorian legacy

This binary thinking about work-as-distinct-from-play is not easily overturned. As well as being a powerful legacy of the industrial economic order of things, it is a resilient way of thinking produced from a strong moral–ethical tradition of Protestant high seriousness. Life, according to this tradition, is essentially about dutiful suffering for which one will be rewarded in a future time and place. This 'call to seriousness', as historian Ian Bradley calls it, had a special appeal to the growing middle classes of the mid-nineteenth century, particularly 'civil servants, officers in the Armed services, bankers, merchants and members of the professions'.[2]

The qualities that gave the British middle classes their competitive edge – industriousness, thrift, self-denial, punctuality, order – were explicitly pitted against the idleness, self-gratification, arbitrariness and excess that marked an aristocracy on the wane. Unlike the monarchs who preceded her, Queen Victoria allied herself squarely with the former values and eschewed the latter, and with good reason. Middle-class values would be the means by which street urchins would be turned into shopkeepers, louts into lawyers, truants into taxpayers. And this – at least in theory – would 'trickle down' into prosperity – and greater moral virtue – for all.

Middle-class Victorians were as corseted in their preference for structure and order as their clothing suggests. This is not to deny the inventive genius which marked that highly successful entrepreneurial era. However, their furrowed brows, their suspicion of pleasure and the precision of the clock marked a firm rejection of any predilection for game-playing. And nowhere was this more in evidence than in the education system that prepared the nation's children for the world of industrial work. Alvin Toffler, writing in his classic prophetic book, *Future Shock*, half a century ago, sums this up succinctly:

> Mass education was the ingenious machine constructed by industrialism to produce the kind of adults it needed. The problem was inordinately complex. How to pre-adapt children for a new world – a world of repetitive indoor toil, smoke, noise, machines, crowded living conditions, collective discipline, a world in which time was to be regulated not by the cycle of the sun and moon, but by the factory whistle and the clock.[3]

Toffler goes on to describe the education system that was to develop as 'an anticipatory mirror' of industrial work, with its regimentation, lack of individualisation, rigid systems of seating, grouping, grading and testing, all in the context of an authoritarian 'boss' teacher.[4] The ecology of the classroom was a perennial lesson in regimentation. With 'a place for everything and everything in its place', it exemplified the triumph of order and Protestant asceticism over serendipity and self-indulgence.

The factory model of schooling has taught post-Victorian generations that a preparation for work involves learning to eschew temporary gratification and to tolerate – indeed to welcome – repetitive and routine experiences in the expectation that these habits will lead to long-term job security, which in turn will bring in turn economic and social prosperity. It has also taught them that schools produce drop-outs as well as credentialled workers, and this is a legacy that lingers today. Just as the factory self-propelled conveyer belt process makes it easier to identify and eliminate product failures, so too the lock-step, sorting and credentialling processes of industrial model schools make it easier to spot and reject underperforming students. As the 'raw materials' of the educational factory, children can be channelled into 'streams' – academic, general, vocational – that can delimit their life chances from then on.

We know that disadvantaged kids are much more likely to be the 'rejects', because they are unlikely to share the values of their teachers or to crack the codes of correct speech and behaviour. As American educationist Julia Steiny dramatically puts it, 'Factory model schools are soul-killers for students and teachers alike. They manufacture student disaffection. And they burn teachers to a crisp.'[5]

Despite the ruthless efficiency of the school in sorting and grading many disadvantaged children out of education, the ability to imitate the routines needed in a predictable and stable social and economic order was nevertheless a way to get out of the dirt and drudgery that were the lot of the working classes – the Great Unwashed – and into the middle or professional classes, with their superior pay and conditions, as well as their 'superior' moral sensibilities. It was the professional classes – doctors, lawyers, accountants, engineers – whose knowledge, in the form of theoretical, applied and analytic skill, would be extolled, valued and rewarded throughout the twentieth century. Elevated above others in the workforce, professional workers knew that their status depended on their work being differentiated from that of manual labourers by its cerebral and orderly nature – work that kept hands out of the dirt and minds on the serious business of doing business. Above all, it was high-minded work, the antithesis of frivolous or menial activity. And it built an empire upon which the sun never set.

It is not an easy thing, therefore, for post-Victorian generations to imagine the blurring of professional and non-professional work, just as it is difficult for post-Victorian generations to imagine creativity as a key economic driver. Having buried the aristocracy's penchant for self-serving pleasures, we find it difficult to come to terms with the idea that professional work might be both pleasurable and creative. The spectre of Blake's dark satanic mills, the undifferentiated greyness of Marcuse's 'one-dimensional man', the narrow-shouldered pen-pusher who stereotypically evokes the ubiquitous public servant – all of these images of professionals at work make it difficult to imagine that mainstream work can and should involve imaginative play, or that today's workers are no longer stereotypically grey-suited men commuting to the CBD with briefcase in hand for eight hours a day, five days a week. In metaphorical terms, the 'suit' remains deeply embedded in our vision of the professional working life.

Suit yourself?

Meanwhile, there is burgeoning evidence that the workplace is an environment undergoing radical change. Wearing a suit is no longer *the* marker of class or status distinctions in the workplace – or at least it should not be, according to workplace analyst Michael Devine. Devine speaks out against what he calls 'hat behaviour': the accoutrements that mark a divisive caste system in the workplace and 'ghettoize ... creative talent' rather than integrating creative thinkers at all levels into the mainstream organisational culture.[6] The predominant metaphor for understanding value has shifted from vertical chains of supply and demand to horizontal networks. Devine argues that in this new order of things, hierarchies of command and control are more likely to frustrate value-added activity than enable it. This does not mean an end to taking leaderly responsibility in the workplace. What it does mean is that leadership is about providing direction and support, rather than taking command and control. It works best when dispersed among all the activities that make up the organisation, not just action 'at the top'.

While some organisations continue to be marked by the overt trappings of rank, radical changes in the economy arising from innovation have for some time now been blurring vertical hierarchies in the workplace. New technology and cultural forms are producing, and being produced by, new forms of capital. Chief among these, and available throughout an entire organisation, is creative capital: the human ingenuity and high-level problem-solving skill that leads to fresh opportunities, ideas, products and modes of social engagement. Writing in *Harvard Business Review*, Richard Florida and Jim Goodnight are emphatic on this point: 'A company's most important asset isn't raw materials, transportation systems, or political influence. It's creative capital – simply put, an arsenal of creative thinkers whose ideas can be turned into valuable products and services.'[7]

Creative capital exists at every level of an organisation. This means that the creative workforce is not limited to computer 'geeks' or suited executives, but is best understood as being distributed throughout a profession and/or an organisation. Salespersons are a source of creative capital when they enrol their customers in productive social relationships that provide timely and authentic feedback about the products they are producing and might produce. Teachers are a source of creative capital when they develop powerful peer-to-peer engagement processes that enhance their students' learning. Public servants are a source of creative capital when they engage in the sort of strategic planning that streamlines staff support and career development opportunities. It is not positioning the hierarchy but human capability in all its ingenious forms that is the essence of creative capital, and it is creative capital that is being heralded – not just by Richard Florida but also by many other academics – as the most valuable asset of the 21st-century organisation.[8]

That being said, there is no doubt that digital technology has aided and abetted creative capital in unprecedented ways. Computer-centred networks and their capabilities have powerfully influenced social systems and social relationships, so much so that, as Manuel Castells points out, we can no longer speak of the 'social' without speaking of the 'technological'.[9] However, the impacts of digital technologies may or may not result in a new or improved set of social dynamics. Futures analyst Saskia Sassen argues that digital technology cannot be depended on to produce new dynamics – they may well be simply derivative or reproduce existing social relations.[10] It is when the best of human ingenuity and the affordances of digital technology are combined that creative capital is generated to do its best work.

The digital economy and the creative industries

While 'going digital' is not of itself any guarantee of entrepreneurial success, there is now ample evidence that the digital industries are providing a model for transforming enterprise culture and the culture of work. With a 100 per cent annual growth rate sustained over twenty-five years, the digital industries are seeing the interaction of market and non-market entities in a co-evolutionary process that connects garages, households and markets without relying on central control as a source of incentive or an organiser of trade.

According to Australian economist John Quiggan, the digital industries are difficult to monetarise, but there is no doubt about their spectacular growth (despite the dot.com crash of 2000–02), nor their increasingly household-driven character.[11] The household-driven innovation in the twenty-first century is, he argues, very different from the consumer passivity that characterised households in the second half of the twentieth century. Like many of its 21st-century counterparts, Web 2.0 action emanates predominantly from households rather than being commercially driven. This means that much of the enterprise is in the 'long tail' of distribution, not in the more recognisable entities like Yahoo, eBay, You Tube or My Space.

A number of social and work-related effects flow from the new dynamics of digital content creation and dissemination. Beyond their capacity to blur class distinctions and workplace hierarchies, they also blur distinctions between production and consumption, labour and citizenship, and commercial and non-commercial enterprise. Digitalisation makes enterprise much less about routinised labour, centrally located offices and 9-to-5ism, and much more about understanding, developing and maintaining the dispositions and conditions that people need to turn symbolic knowledge into economic and social assets.

The 'creative industries' are exemplary locations of this type of enterprise. They are industries that exist for a wide range of purposes, from creative design and construction to innovation in the social and human services, and they include, but are not limited to, media and the visual and performing arts. Although they obviously do not have a monopoly on 'creativity' – the creative workforce is not concentrated in one creative ghetto but rather is highly integrated across the economy – they can nevertheless be shown to be highly innovative not only in terms of artistic expression but also in terms of business models, modes of organising, integration of technology, and formulation of new products and services.[12] Their stock-in-trade is the exploitation of symbolic knowledge and skills, not only through artistic works but also through adding value and marketing. In this sense, they combine commercial knowledge and application with aesthetic modes of knowing and doing.

Creative industries are knowledge-intensive industries that require highly skilled human capital.[13] They are strategically important enablers as intermediate inputs to other industry sectors, with the economic multipliers into other economic sectors (that is, productivity and employment growth per dollar invested) being higher for the creative industries than for most other categories of economic activity.[14] This has been established empirically for at least one state economy in Australia, namely Queensland.[15]

Data provided by the Queensland University of Technology's Creative Industries Faculty indicates that, in April 2006,[16] there were 55,000 creative enterprises registered with the Australian Taxation Office, representing 6.6 per cent of the total number of GST-registered enterprises in operation. Alongside those enterprises, there were 253,000 creative enterprises without GST registration, mostly sole practitioners, representing 10.8 per cent of the total non-GST-registered enterprises. This means that more than 5 per cent of Australia's workforce, or nearly half a million people, were employed in the creative industries, with another 2 per cent of Australia's workers also contributing to the overall 'creative economy'. The digital creative industries have generated $A21 billion, with nearly $15 billion of that being contributed directly from the creative industries.

According to Edna del Santos, chief of the United Nations Creative Industries Program (UNCTAD), United Kingdom revenues from trade and intellectual property in the visual and performing arts, publishing, traditional knowledge (arts and crafts) music, design, new media and audiovisuals added 1.8 million jobs and $US11.6 billion or 4 per cent balance of trade in 2004. In Denmark in 2003, 5.3 per cent GDP and 16 per cent of exports were attributable to the creative industries.[17] Because of the growing demand for communicative technology – 24 per cent of China's exports are now in high-technology products – the prognosis for these industries alone is that exponential growth will continue unabated. Indeed, British economic analyst John Howkins predicts that workers in these industries will be worth $6.1 trillion by 2010.[18]

Growth in the creative industries is predicated not only on digitalisation but also on sustainable futures. Dwindling fossil fuel supplies and concerns about our current patterns of energy consumption have given rise to radical rethinking in resource-rich communities that are looking over the horizon to plan for a collective future when the resources run out. One such community is Cobar, in New South Wales, a mining town that employed an economic development pioneer, Ernesto Sirolli, to assist it to set up a program of economic diversification. Sirolli's picture of Cobar as a post-mining community is very much focused on creative capacity building: 'I think it will be absolutely possible to have a very new generation of entrepreneurs and entrepreneurial activities being ready to absorb and to create jobs when the mine was closed, so I think it's a very, very smart idea to start to look at your economy when you're still okay.'[19]

The key point about pre-empting an 'over the horizon' future for Cobar or any other similar community is the recognition that it will need to be invented: there is no prescription or template from the past that can be relied upon to deliver the products and services on which this community's future will depend. They will be produced by the creative smarts of entrepreneurs who are now in kindergartens and primary schools, not just in New South Wales but also in India, China and Singapore – indeed, no country is too far from the entrepreneurial action, if the capacities of its citizens are relevant and the demand is high.

Few of those who will be engaged in the entrepreneurial activities that will characterise a 'post-mining boom ' town like Cobar will actually live in Cobar. This is so because many of the services that will sustain such a community will involve well-educated, highly skilled workers working in offshore or interstate locations.

Meanwhile, much of the work being done by low-skill workers with basic education will be automated or moved offshore. This will leave a few low-wage, personal service jobs such as babysitting, garbage collection, security services and street cleaning, and one or two better-paid skilled jobs like carpentry, plumbing and electrical services, to be done by and for locals in the community. Such jobs will still be needed, but they will not be the jobs on which the new entrepreneurial future of such a community will be based, and they will continue to be vulnerable to automation and/or offshoring.

It is important to note here that the list of jobs we traditionally associate with 'personal services' is not stable nor is it immune from being moved offshore to a low-wage country. While we have not yet seen a dramatic increase in the number of paid services being moved offshore, the trend in the USA to move low-end service work to low-wage earners in India and China is characteristic of a growing worldwide trend to shift whatever work can be shifted to low-wage countries. What this will mean, according to American economist Alan Binder, is that the category 'personal service' will be increasingly vulnerable to 'offshoring'.[20] It will not just be low-level 'impersonal' service providers like call centre operators who will experience job vulnerability. Personal services like preparing tax returns or civil engineering may well become partly if not entirely offshore-able. Binder insists that the increasing reach of technology will have a profound impact on those jobs we have thought to be 'personal':

> Traditionally we think of service jobs as being largely immune to foreign competition. After all, you can't get your hair cut or your broken arm

set by a barber or doctor in a distant land. But stunning advances in communication technology, plus the vast new labour pool in Asia and Eastern Europe, are changing that picture radically, subjecting millions of presumed-safe domestic jobs to foreign competition. And it is not necessary actually to move jobs to low-wage countries in order to restrain wage increases; the mere threat of offshoring can put a damper on wages.[21]

The work that will be least vulnerable to 'offshoring' is high-end personal service: heart surgery, divorce law and so on. This sort of service requires, in turn, highly educated and highly skilled workers who are adept at using advanced technology and in interacting with clients to service their needs. High-end impersonal services such as writing computer code and statistical analysis likewise demand high levels of education and a capacity to utilise cutting-edge technology to solve problems, create new products and communicate in efficient and effective ways.

It is not easy for young people who are used to high standards of living and relatively stable economic and social circumstances to come to terms with the profound implications of a genuinely global and highly competitive labour market. As John Young, founder of the US Council on Competitiveness, has remarked, 'Our standard of living is not a birthright. We have to earn it in the marketplace every day.'[22] This means that the twentieth-century neocolonial map many of us carry in our heads about wealth and poverty – about who is at the cutting edge of innovation and who is not – is radically out of date. The dominance of the USA and Europe in scientific and technological innovation is being challenged by such countries as India, Korea, Singapore, Taiwan and China. The skill levels needed to gain competitive advantage are high – as high as the levels of risk involved and the new employment opportunities being generated.

What do employers want?

The key point here is that a high level of education – at least a university undergraduate degree or equivalent – is necessary but not sufficient to be highly employable in such a climate. Communicative and interpersonal interaction, digital savvy and design or aesthetic skills are all crucial to providing high-end personal services. And this makes trouble for the idea that success in the holy trinity of 'English, maths and science' is the key to future employment success.

Many employers indicate that, when it comes to short-listing of applicants for a professional position, the level of education is a 'tick box' or credentialling matter.[23] Without it, there will be no short-listing. But it does not guarantee anything at all beyond this. When hundreds of applications are received for a single position in a law firm, for example, the real competition starts after the tick-box credential issue relegates those few who have 'almost finished' their degree to the bin.

So what are employers looking for beyond the formal credential? According a recent report of the UK Higher Education Academy, 'employability' – the combination of a person's achievements and potential to obtain paid work – is achieved through complex learning that includes not only disciplinary learning but also 'generic' or transferable capacities that can map on to an employing organisation's vision or strategy.[24] Put another way, employability in both high-end personal and impersonal services involves two kinds of expertise, one of which derives from a particular field of knowledge that is the focus of an undergraduate degree, and one that is about deploying such knowledge and understanding to optimal effect.

Those individuals who possess this combination of skills are highly employable as 'symbolic analysts': the imaginative and creative thinkers who build the capacity of an organisation to compete in a highly demanding economic environment.

A symbolic analyst adds value to an entrepreneurial organisation through their capacity to:

⤳ theorise and/or relate empirical data or other forms of evidence using formulae and equations as well as innovative models and metaphors

⤳ see the part in the context of the wider and more complex whole

⤳ intuitively or analytically experiment with ideas and their products

↳ collaborate with others in ways that increase opportunities for successful innovation.[25]

These capacities demand more than basic communication, literacy and numeracy skills. They also demand more than a capacity to use information technology. And this runs counter to the idea that 'core work skills' have not changed beyond those so loved and cherished by 'back to basics' advocates. Neither 'back to basics' nor the 'shelter effect' of staying longer in formal education will of themselves be guarantees of employability. Being educated is crucial, but it is the kind of educational experience rather than the number of years spent in formal education that makes the real difference for engaging successfully in the higher-order analysis that is needed in 21st-century workplaces.

The importance of 'better; not just more' education is a strong theme of the recent report from the US National Center on Education and the Economy, *Tough Choices or Tough Times*. The argument is put early and often in the report that more of the same education will not be sufficient to equip American youth for their 21st-century working futures. Not only will they, like Australian young people, have to 'participate in work teams that are truly global'[26] but also they will find that many of the routine jobs once available in abundance no longer exist. The report stresses that 'over the horizon' work requires a powerful disposition to learn far beyond one specific trade and to draw on much more than one discipline. It says:

> Line workers who cannot contribute to the design of the products they are fabricating may be as obsolete as the last model of that product … auto mechanics will have to figure out what to do when many of the computers in the cars they are working on do not function as they were designed to function … software engineers who are also musicians and artists will have an edge over those who are not as the entertainment industry evolves [and] it will pay architects to know something about nanotechnology and small business people who build custom yachts and fishing boats will be able to survive only if they quickly learn a lot about the scientific foundations of carbon fiber composites.[27]

Of course, it is one thing to accept that the capacities of a creative workforce are broad in their scope and deep in their level of thinking and doing, but it is another to understand precisely what they are and how they might be fostered both within and outside formal learning education. A great deal of work has been done by policy-makers to identify these capacities. The strength and the limitation of much of this work is the extent to which it seeks to demystify what is needed. The provision of long and detailed lists of work-related skills and capacities such as appear in documents like the Australian Commonwealth Government–funded *Employability Skills for the Future* serves both to illuminate and to atomise the dispositions to learning and engagement that are the bedrock of employability into the creative workforce.[28] Simply put, we can miss the woods for the trees.

A number of skill groupings have become relatively predictable in such documents nevertheless, which is an indication of the consistency with which employers are responding to the question of what they are seeking in an employee. In *Employability Skills for the Future*, skills and attributes are clustered under the following unsurprising headings: personal attributes (such as motivation and adaptability), communication (such as empathising and, increasingly, speaking in languages other than English, teamwork, initiative and enterprise (including 'being creative'), problem-solving (such as 'developing creative, innovative solutions'), planning and organising, self-management (including intellectual property), life-long learning and familiarity with technology.

In relation to the last of these categories – technology – it needs to be understood that the level of technological skill compatible with the needs of the creative workforce is much higher than the basic ability to use a computer for generating Word documents, using email and simple internet searches. The managing director of the global recruitment firm Manpower has pointed out that 'you need to be comfortable with IT … whether you are using keyboards or hand-held devices because information will come to you through technology'.[29] Moreover, as the complexity of technology increases, new models of collaboration will also become more complex, demanding greater speed and scope from teams of workers using digital tools to collaborate across boundaries – organisational, disciplinary, demographic and regional.

Boundary-crossing from school to work and back again is already a feature of the lives of many young people still in post-compulsory schooling. Such life experience can make a useful contribution to alleviating difficulties inherent in developing employability skills in the classroom. However, it is no cure-all, and may also have negative effects, depending on the type of work being done and the relationship – if any – between the school, the workplace and the home.

We know already that engaging in study and work in parallel is not always a positive experience. Many of the tasks young people do in 'work experience' jobs are as routine, functional and repetitive as many of the tasks they are asked to perform at school, providing few opportunities for engaging creatively with complexity. While low-level personal service jobs may well be available, many young people are looking for opportunities to work in environments that will allow them a lifestyle that blurs the distinction between their work world and their personal interests, as discussed in chapter 1.

Employer organisations that are aware of this trend know the importance of acknowledging it and capitalising on it. A report to the Australian Industry Group in May 2006 makes this explicit as a vision of the possible 'big shifts' in business organisations: 'Workers are look-ing for more opportunities for self-expression. They will increasingly focus on their hobbies and other leisure-time activities. As they try to bring these "passions" into the workplace, leading-edge companies are looking for ways to incorporate worker interests into formal job descriptions.'[30]

At the same time as progressive employers expect that the work-place will need to be customised to accommodate such expectations, they also have an expectation that their employees will exhibit, within this more customised environment, a capacity for judicious self-man-agement, including a well-developed ability to be self-critical. This is not so easily developed in a schooling culture that values external affirmation more than tough self-management (see chapter 5). Nor is it easily managed by employers who find their young employees happy to receive feedback – but only if it is positive!

Shifting from coercion to self-management

All this renegotiation of workplace roles and responsibilities is part of a larger cultural shift away from a command and control ethic – in business, school and family life – towards self-motivation and self-management, whereby people act on their own behalf, eschewing intermediaries, templates and hierarchies in favour of self-fashioning according to personal needs, desires and belief systems. It brings with it more responsibility – and more risk – at a time when young people in Western cultures have never been more protected from the negative impact of risk on their lives.

While exposure to risk-taking may be a deficit in the life experiences of the Yuk/Wow Generation of workers, they will come with numerous advantages over previous generations. As explained in chapter 2, most will be more digitally literate, more capable of multitasking and more globally connected, team-oriented and open to diversity, difference and sharing than their parents and teachers. They are more interested in being part of 'kid-to-kid' networks in which they have 'hands on, plugged in' engagement.

This is the sort of activity that characterises how 'gamers' learn, according to a large research study conducted in the USA by John Beck and Mitchell Wade.[31] They show that 'gamers' are much more likely than their baby boomer predecessors to jump over preambles and introductions and much less anxious in the absence of top-down rules. Moreover, as Beck and Wade found, the gamer environment is not an unregulated environment, but gamers have 'systematically different ways of working ... systematically different skills to learn, and different ways to learn them'.[32] They learn to use a meta-map or to operate without one, rather than learning from instruction from 'outside' the subculture.

As future workers, young people with learning preferences of this sort are not likely to remain long in a workplace that is over-managed, inflexible or hierarchical. Employers for whom compliance matters above all else will have difficulty retaining such young people. Already anecdotal evidence from industry suggests that many employers are frustrated about what they perceive as a lack of 'stickability' in many young employees, and are in turn ambivalent about investing in training them if they have been 'burnt' by trainees who lasted just a few weeks or even a few days on the job. A healthy and robust employment market, while desirable for a host of other reasons, can exacerbate this situation.

We do know that long-term continuous engagement in study or work is becoming a thing of the past for many of these young people. The trend to 'early departure' is becoming a feature of undergraduate education, with many more students opting out or delaying entry than in previous times. This is a characteristic of the 75 per cent of American undergraduates categorised by the US National Centre for Educational Statistics as 'non-traditional'. To be categorised as 'non-traditional', undergraduates have delayed enrolment, attend part-time, work full-time while enrolled, are financially independent, have dependants, are single parents or lack a high school diploma.[33] In other words, being non-traditional – taking multiple pathways and refusing linear continuity – is becoming the norm.

For the Yuk/Wow Generation, the norm is to be on the move. This expectation of immediacy of connection and instant gratification is one that is not easily addressed by parents, teachers or employers. The Yuk/Wows, intolerant as they are of delay, will have a greater propensity to become frustrated when held apart from what they want, no matter how apparently short the time-span or trivial the issue. A request on Monday morning is sent in the expectation of a reply that same hour, let alone that same morning. 'Staying in the grey' or 'letting things come' are not valued life strategies, regardless of their value to others.

However, while 'have it all and have it now' might be understandable as a logic for living in a speeded-up world, the onus on employers to provide a safe environment, and to ensure that employees have the skills necessary to work optimally within that environment, is inevitably a constraint that might not be well received. Moreover, recent research into how creativity is enabled or obstructed in the workplace has indicated that, while tight deadlines can in certain circumstances move workers to produce more creative solutions, time pressure usually works against creative outcomes. Put another way, 'When creativity is under the gun, it usually ends up being killed.'[34]

If, as argued in the opening chapter, the creative process often involves combining ideas that are not normally associated with each other, then this takes time – time to juggle and to play with combinations, perhaps to reject all combinations and start again. When time pressures build up and workplace distractions increase, it can become virtually impossible to gain and hold a focus long enough to generate a creative solution to a problem. This was a finding of a study of time pressure and creativity conducted by an American multi-university research team that surveyed 177 employees of twenty-two project teams from seven US companies in three types of industry: chemical, high tech and consumer products.[35] This study of work patterns and preferences, focused as it was on those considered the 'creative lifeblood' of the organisation, found that creativity seemed more likely when people were able to focus on a single activity for most of the day.

In broad terms, creative outputs were found to be much less likely where people were on autopilot, getting little encouragement for their managers and being required to attend formal meetings at the expense of time spent engaging collaboratively with individuals who share their passions. Workers who experience the sort of time pressure that had them feeling 'as if they are on a treadmill' were highly unlikely to experience the positive challenge or to be able to maintain the focus that creativity demands.

Such issues demand sensitive negotiation in an organisation bent upon harnessing the most creative outputs of its workers and its working environment. They are unlikely to be resolved by authoritarian behaviour on the part of employers or disengagement on the part of employees. Nor can managers simply wish time pressures away. One strategy that is useful, however, is to work on minimising interruptions, distractions and unrelated demands, including the 'meeting mania' that is so often a feature of the daily life of formal organisations. Despite all that has been said about the waste of time and money that can result from regular meeting schedules, the perennial meeting

– with its agendas and roles set in advance – is still sacrosanct in many large organisations. Meanwhile, the real action is likely to be happening elsewhere.

Leadership that builds creativity

There are real implications of all this for workforce leadership. Bill Martin, consultant to business and educational organisations seeking cultural change, has a useful conceptual model for making the culture shifts necessary to build creative capacity throughout the workplace.[36] He argues that there are five levels of organisational activity that need to be attended to, and he presents these in a hierarchy of importance, starting with Vision and working downwards to Mental Models, Systemic Organisation, Behaviours and Events.

The top three – Vision (the shared sense of purpose in an organisation), Mental Models (the hard-wired beliefs people have about the organisation and their role within it) and Systemic Organisation (the way activity is organised in terms of time and place) – are the areas that Martin believes should occupy the vast bulk of a leader's time and attention. Indeed Martin argues that 85 per cent of a leader's time and attention should be focused on these three meta-issues for the organisation.

Behaviours (such as how people engage with the work and each other from moment to moment) and Events (deadlines, meetings, seminars, hiring, performance reviews, social rituals and so on) should occupy only 15 per cent of a leader's time. Martin argues that the reverse is actually true of most organisations. That is, leaders spend far too much time micromanaging behaviour and events that occur in the work culture and far too little time working on meta-issues that frame the work culture.

It is not that leaders choose to do this perversely – many capable leaders find their attention dragged into the daily push and pull of organisational decision-making and the extent to which organisations begin to feed off themselves. An apparently useful set of activities – for example, regular performance and planning reviews – can all too easily become straitjacketed by compliance rather than being an opportunity to invite people in all areas of the organisation to contribute to the meta-activity that drives and sustains the culture. Greg Goodman is one of many highly successful business leaders who does not get caught in bureaucracy. As described in *Boss* magazine, Goodman's approach to management captures the sort of attitude and disposition that characterise successful corporate leaders in these highly competitive and demanding times. He is 'in the trenches with his troops [and hates] hierarchy'.[37] Goodman insists that his staff do not work for him but with him, and he places a strong emphasis on knowing his staff, a considerable task given that he has more than thirty offices around the globe. He is both passionate about his work and the people who work with him:

> [His] real passion is for building the business. He wants his enjoyment of doing property deals and setting up property funds to filter across the company, and encourages networks of staff to spring up from within the group. The business he has built up keeps expanding at a rapid rate, and there is no sign that Goodman is slowing down. 'You've got to be moving forward,' he says. 'There is no place in the marketplace to be in a holding pattern.'[38]

The pleasure of the work is clearly a key motivation for Goodman. It is what sustains him and motivates him to keep up a very heavy schedule of travel and fuels his determination to with – rather than on – his employees. Pleasure, like risk-taking, is not something that can be legislated. It needs to be brought into being from day to day and week to week. This is one reason why so little attention is given to degrees of pleasure or risk – they cannot be easily planned for, nor are they amenable to measurement. The adage that 'if it can't be measured, it doesn't count' has become so powerful as a driver of the logic of organisational activity that pleasure and risk continue to struggle to be seen or heard as valuable indicators of a successful workplace.

Much can be learned from the rituals indigenous people use to express their valuing of each other and their pleasure in coming together as a community. In New Zealand, working Maori women understand the importance of bringing to the workplace the food they have prepared and sharing it in a space they 'own' at work for this purpose. Notwithstanding the importance of these rituals to those who partake of them, they still sit outside the 'serious' business of getting on with the 'real' work, a legacy of our Anglo forebears that we could well do without.

It is difficult to feel valued when it is widely perceived that the only opinions that really count are those of senior management. And it is difficult for senior managers to redress this perception when they are busy engaging with each other and closely focused on guarding against any and all potential pitfalls for the organisation. The larger the organisation, the more likely it is that hyper-rational systems of audit and accountability will win out over engaging with what people are thinking and doing in reality.

The risky business of risk management

Almost a century ago, the British author G. K. Chesterton said that life is not illogical but that it is 'a trap for logicians'.[39] This means we can predict that systematic planning and rational management will serve most people's needs most of the time. Yet there will always be a gap between systems and people because people are 'nearly reasonable' while systems are totally reasonable. The implications of this remark do not seem to be well understood by the management of many post-millennial organisations, despite all the rhetoric about people being the most important organisational resource, and despite all the evidence we now have that risk-taking is as necessary to sustaining a robust work culture as risk minimising.

In highly risk-conscious organisations, many employees find themselves torn between paying attention to tasks to which they need to apply their skill or expertise and applying their organisational knowledge as 'expert' managers of systems. This push-and-pull changes the nature of what we come to value as professional work. For social management theorists Richard Ericson and Kevin Haggerty, a key part of the work of modern professionals is to translate their 'know-how' into 'expertise' in their organisation. It is not enough to be competent in your 'craft'; as an employee you must learn the jargon for communicating this competence in and for the organisational system. They say: '[P]rofessionals obviously have "know-how" [but] their "know-how" does not become expertise until it is plugged into an institutional communication system. It is through such systems that expert knowledge becomes standardized and robust enough to use in routine diagnosis, classification, and treatment decisions by professionals.'[40]

There is value in sharing an organisational language. There is danger when its codes are understood and spoken by only a lofty few. Where the information flow is exclusively in the hands of senior managers, many employees will miss the opportunity to learn from and contribute to the knowledge that sustains the organisation. 'Mining the anthill' of creative capacity demands explicit invitations to all staff to contribute ideas, and this requires, in turn, that sufficient information is provided to all staff to allow everyone to 'crack the code'. Without this, policies requiring 'inclusive representation' are gestural at best. A member of staff can sit at any number of meetings and at any level, but if the talk is all 'in code' they will learn only that they are not part of the conversation.

Why is inclusivity so important? Because, as we have learned from 'change' research, one or two 'champions' are not likely to shift an entire culture. Nor is one leader – no matter how personally impressive – capable of knowing or deciding what to do at any given time. Without explicit processes for mining all the ideas and capabilities that exist throughout the organisation, too few are being asked to do the thinking for far too many, and it is unfair on both. Perhaps more importantly, it is a waste of the resources for which everyone is being paid.

Shifting a culture away from exclusiveness, compliance and joylessness to inclusivity, risk-taking and joyfulness is not easy. It is not easy because of the weight of the Victorian work legacy, still so much in evidence in our schools, the deep-seated Anglo mistrust of fun and pleasure, the misrecognition of compliance as the beginning and end of performance, and the incredible resilience of practices that worked well for us in another time and place.

Put simply, people are pretty hard-wired when it comes to change.

Anglo males are unlikely to want to cook food for their fellow employees. Highly passive students are unlikely to turn into highly active workers if they experience work as a continuation of school. Employees who have been victims of mean-spiritedness in their workplace are unlikely to be generous in the way they enact their role.

So what?

So what can be done? Two large-scale research studies of 'great managers' conducted by the Gallup Organisation found that 'breaking all the rules' of conventional wisdom was a necessary starting point for effective leadership.[41] The study synthesised its findings about the approach taken by good managers in the following four simple propositions:

People don't change that much.

Don't waste time trying to put in what was left out.

Try to draw out what was left in.

That is hard enough.[42]

This implies that a leader's unseemly rush to 'break the furniture' of orthodox practice can be as unproductive as ignoring poor performance and hoping it will somehow improve with time. Where a leader has been rewarded for their long-term performance record of staying well inside the safe boundaries of organisational routines and rituals, it is highly unlikely that there will be any signal 'from above' that more creativity will be valued in the workplace. Where they have been rewarded for experimenting and make mistakes, in order to bring value-adding perspectives and ways of operating to the workplace, they are more likely to value others who do likewise.

Good managers will signal strongly what it is they value, and that will be borne out in whom or what they pay attention to. And this will be evident in the design and culture of the workplace as well as in the attitudes and dispositions of employees. Where staff members avoid eye-contact with each other and with clients, where the printers and photocopiers are perennially out of order, where boxes pile up in the corner and the pot-plants have died, it is likely that the people will be similarly dysfunctional, hunkered down and flat.

Edicts from above, dire threats and special pleading are not particularly helpful. The message needs to be clear that in this work culture much is expected and much is given in support. We know quite a lot about the life preferences of future employees, through the leisure activities they enjoy and the way they choose to learn. It is not a simple matter of endorsing all these preferences and modes of engagement and accommodating them all in the workplace. The imperative is to learn from them in order to optimise the opportunities they provide us with for building a more creative work culture.

Education: important and irrelevant

How should we think about the role formal of education in terms of preparing the creative workforce? Put bluntly, schools and universities are more important and less relevant than ever. Indeed, many commentators argue that schooling kills creativity stone dead. Yet we know that education is crucial to improving our life chances. What are we to make of this conundrum?

We know education is more important because of the weight of evidence that a more highly educated population means a better lifestyle, a bigger pay packet and a more productive economy. There is no doubt about this as a fact of social and economic life.[1] We also know that that 'creatives' need to have high levels of traditional literacy and numeracy if they are to function at a high level in a complex economic and social order. According to a recent report from the USA's National Center on Education and the Economy: 'This is a world in which a very high level of preparation in reading, writing, speaking mathematics, science, literature, history, and the arts will be an indispensable foundation for everything that comes after for most members of the workforce.'[2]

Why are academic skills still needed?

As social scientist Mark Warschauer points out,[3] we live in paradoxical times (variously described as the Late Age of Print[4] or the Post-Typographic Society[5]) in which information literacy still depends to a large extent on print literacy. He asserts that 'competence in traditional literacies is often a gateway to successful entry into the world of new literacies',[6] citing American high school research into student use of computers and the internet in defence of this claim. In doing so, he refutes the 'romantic notion' that many reform advocates have of the 'empowering potential of learning and new media' in and of itself. It is not enough, Warschauer argues, to be able to create multimedia presentations with the latest digital tools or to spend most of one's time in front of a computer screen.

This is corroborated by the OECD finding that, while more experience with computer use is valuable, more frequent use does not necessarily lead to better performance. The PISA Study of computer use found that moderate users performed better than students who were either not using computers, using them rarely or using computers very often.[7]

While the capacities associated with 'going digital' are useful and important, they are insufficient to creative workforce capacity. They can even be counter-productive if they are relied on to take the place of super-complex thinking. High levels of literacy – both traditional and digital – are needed, and neither can do it alone.

A further point needs to be made here. It should not be assumed that because a young person is highly digitally literate, they therefore know how to optimise digital technology for academic purposes. A key conclusion of a University of Melbourne Study[8] concurs with the findings of a US study[9] of freshman students: that many first-year students

The creative workforce

struggle not to make technology work *per se* but to make it work for academic ends:

> It is not that first year students are incapable of using technology for specialized, context-appropriate purposes; indeed many would have recently had these experiences at school. The critical point is that while [they] might use technology in a range of ways and may, apparently, be digitally literate, we cannot assume that being a member of the 'Net' Generation is synonymous with knowing how to employ technology-based tools strategically to optimise learning experiences and outcomes ...[10]

Why more of the same education won't work

The foundational competencies of reading, writing, speaking, mathematics, science, literature, history and the arts are more likely than digital literacy to be developed within classrooms, just as they have been for a couple of centuries. This fact acknowledged, it is also necessary to face the uncomfortable truth about the increasing irrelevance of schools to the patterns of life and work in the twenty-first century. The NCEE report *Tough Choices or Tough Times* makes this abundantly clear: '[The twenty-first century] is a world in which comfort with ideas and abstractions is the passport to a good job, in which creativity and innovation are the keys to the good life, in which high levels of education – *a very different kind of education than most of us have had* – are going to be the only security there is [my emphasis].'[11]

Put another way, a better education cannot mean more of the same education. The glossy brochures and syllabus preambles of formal education keep promising to help young people reach their full potential while schooling and tertiary education continue to deliver much that has little to do with their futures, or indeed the future of learning. Rigour is *de rigueur* for these 21st-century times. As argued in chapter 6, we have been in retreat from rigour for some time, fearing that its effect on the self-esteem of vulnerable young people might be damaging, and signing off on 'easy success' and instant opinion-making as more appropriate to developing minds. 'Having fun with maths' is not the same as being introduced to the pleasures and affordances of numerical thinking. Fun is important, but of itself it is unlikely to result in a sustained passion for problem-solving and a willingness to wrestle with ambiguity and complexity. It may be a starting point on the journey, but too often we see 'having fun' collapse into reiterations of low-level tasks that come with low learning expectations, and inevitably lead to low achievement.

This is not to argue that theories of teaching and learning have revolved entirely around child happiness and safety in recent decades. We have seen a proliferation of interest in learning styles, special needs, cognitive development and so on. However, schools are by and large still organised through child protection and risk minimisation legislation on the one hand and standard operational procedures produced in the Industrial and Information Ages of the nineteenth and twentieth centuries on the other. They were not designed for the risky learning challenges of what Daniel Pink calls the 'Conceptual Age',[12] the age in which we now live.

Unlike the Information Age, in which the core business was the routine accessing of information to solve routine problems, the Conceptual Age invests in, and springs from, the new cultural forms and modes of consumption that digital tools and new modes of communication are making possible. Whether or not we agree that all this amounts to the first real generation gap since rock and roll, as creativity guru Sir Ken Robinson claims,[13] it certainly makes unique demands of educators, just as it makes unique demands of the systems, strategies and sustainability of organisations.

Educators, and the institutions in which they work, are ill-equipped to meet these demands, either by their professional learning or by the standard infrastructure of educational facilities. The vast majority of schools today (and, indeed, the institutions that train teachers), continue by and large to use structures and artefacts pertinent to the Industrial and Information Ages. In organisational terms, schooling is organised as a top-down hierarchy of command and control, with designated timetables, fragmented and specialised disciplines, and classrooms designed to house thirty or so students with front-facing desks in rows and black- or whiteboards. Moreover, despite the tinkering with curriculum that we have seen in more recent times, teachers continue to work as singular 'content authorities'. And while they do so, the students may well be living in a parallel learning universe.

It's not just about new technology

Whether or not the blackboard has been replaced by a whiteboard, the dominant culture still remains a culture of transmission. This speaks of the resilience and intractability of the experience of being taught, and it extends from preschool right through to doctoral studies. While technologically mediated tools have recently been conspicuously employed, the logic of their usage is predicated on pre-existing transmission-based models of pedagogy. Put another way, technology specifically designed for social interaction may end up doing little more than transmitting information or assisting with the location of websites. Laptop computers, projectors and interactive whiteboards are more likely to stand in for pens and paper, blackboard diagrams and print-based worksheets, despite the efforts of academic staff developers and a small but growing band of innovative teachers, and despite the opportunities they afford for a very different type of introduction to learning. In universities we still see instances of two dominant commercial learning management systems, Blackboard and WebCT (Web Classroom Teaching) being repurposed for old 'transmission' teaching. Without real pedagogical expertise, many teachers remain wedded to the old transmissive habits, and this is true whether or not they have digital technology at their disposal.

Ask schoolchildren to provide a picture of their experience of school, and the picture they are most likely to paint is 'blah blah blah' from the teacher at the front. As I have indicated, information technology may actually exacerbate regression to transmission pedagogy, not encourage alternatives. A recent study of the uptake and usage of digital technology in the UK shows how students experience this:

> It's quite tedious. A lot of the teachers tend to just get the stuff off the internet and read it straight to you. Whereas before they might have

explained it more, and they would have to have used their own words, rather than the internet's words.

I mean with my business teachers, they just go and visit, and copy stuff there, and they read it to you. Whereas I can just go on the internet and do exactly the same. I'm not particularly learning much from them.[14]

The brute message is that young people are not very interested in listening to what old people have to tell them. They don't learn well that way, unless the teacher is exceptionally inspiring and enthusiastic. The command and control model of schooling is still dominant, and this limits the sort of curriculum, pedagogy and assessment that can be enacted in a school. And it persists despite all the gestures towards democratisation we now see in the conduct of everyday school life. It would be understandable if teachers felt miffed by accusations that things have not changed much in schools. There is evidence of substantial change at the periphery – pastoral care is IN, student leadership is IN, parent engagement is IN. Parades and mass assemblies are generally OUT, corporal punishment is OUT, as is sarcasm, ridicule and 'failure'. Speech nights remain for some schools but with a difference – less formal, more celebratory. School formals, sub-formals and rock eisteddfods are IN, allowing young people to try on identities derived from the entertainment industry and the lives of the rich and famous. However, while this might have made schools more interesting spaces for young people to interact in, the fundamentals – lock-step progression, class grouping, memorisation, testing, monitoring and reporting – remain pretty much intact.

It is not a matter of 'blaming' school-based educators for this state of affairs, but it is important to understand the double vision that governments of all persuasions require of teachers. At a time when child protection legislation is central to any government policy related to children, teachers now have an expanded duty of care in which risk of any kind is to be minimised while simultaneously they are expected to provide an open, creative environment that encourages risk-taking. Schools must be on guard against the unfamiliar, the alien as potential danger at the same time as they are supposed to welcome 'openness' to new ideas and modes of thinking. So the sort of risk-taking made possible through opening up schools remains in tension at all times with claims about 'safety first'. The push and pull of risk is a pendulum that swings back and forth in social life, and this is a condition that we all now live with in a 'risk society' (a society in which minimising potential dangers is the fundamental logic of management).[15] So it is not a problem amenable to a solution. We will continue to worry about the dangers of encouraging young children to sit on Santa's knee at the same time we will worry about teaching young people to be fearful rather than outgoing. We want their robustness, yet we fear its consequences.

Making (class)room for creativity

Knowing all this does not assist schools to make a case that they are relevant to the cultural and social norms of the twenty-first century. Richard Florida expressed his negative view of schooling in general in his visit to Australia a few years ago.[16] Florida was responding to questions from an audience of Queensland academics, politicians, bureaucrats and students as an expert on economic growth and social renewal in the USA. He had just finished a presentation about the importance of place in organising the sort of work that is done by the 'creative class'. According to Florida's empirical study of American economic trends, growth requires open systems that value social and cultural difference, technology and talent.[17] Schools, by contrast, continue to operate as closed systems with traditional notions of accountability and performance expertise. Schools, he said, are squelchers.

While admitting that his research has been in economics, not in education, Florida contended that schools are disconnected from the creative workplace and likely to remain so. By implication, preparing the creative class begins either after formal education has done its worst or all around its dead heart. A recent news article entitled 'Restricted room for creativity' reported that Kirpal Singh, a lecturer at a Singapore university, shares Florida's negative view. Each year, he begins by explaining to his new students that the course he teaches in creative thinking is 'to undo the damage that 12 years of schooling have done to you'.[18]

Ken Robinson is equally unequivocal about schools' negative impact on creativity.[19] He argues that we are now paying dearly for continuing to build education systems in the image of the industrial economy and continuing to use analytic tools of the Enlightenment. The mutual dependence of our natural states of being is not, he argues, mirrored in education. We continue to fail to understand or value the process of defeating habit through originality because we use a narrow and dated economic lens to ascribe value. Dynamic cultural systems need a different way of describing, but for Robinson, this is not likely in the current ideology of schooling, with its subject hierarchies (with arts at the bottom) and its predilection for testing the capacity to memorise dated information.

With established populations in decline, and emergent economies growing at an unprecedented rate, the lives of young people are fast becoming much more complex in terms of the issues they face and the choices available to them. We have been monitoring 'learning needs' through special education for some time now, but it may well be that Attention Deficit Disorder is not a disorder but a logical social product of our times. Indeed, it may serve a perverse sort of purpose in relation to living with super-complexity. On the other hand, mass custody, the legal duty of schools, requires the identification and minimisation of the risk of aberrant behaviour, as defined through traditional conceptions of learning.

Perhaps, then, the call to 'open up' to risk-taking and experimentation should just be ignored by those who really understand the nature of schooling and its necessary limitations. If Florida is correct in his assertion that closed systems which operate out of traditional notions of accountability and performance expertise are unlikely to lead to success either in wealth creation or in social renewal, then perhaps we should pull back from asking for creative capacity-building to be taken seriously in schools and universities. If openness to the external world is fundamental to the tolerance, technological savvy and talent that are the attributes of Florida's creative class, and if schools cannot by definition be run as 'open systems', then it may be asking for 'double vision' from our educators.

The narrow performance-based logic of accountability that schools value and pay attention to flies in the face not only of a broad agenda about distributive justice as a human rights issue but also of the logic of economic growth itself. In the rush to get the 'best clients' in the schooling market, school leaders may misrecognise the importance of student and parent diversity as a spur to innovation and change. Moreover, as Guy Claxton points out,[20] our high achievers on narrow test instruments might not be the twenty-first century's most robust and resilient learners, and this has implications for the debate about the value of testing for quality assurance as well as debates about the skill sets that are most relevant to employability. As indicated earlier, brilliantly successful creatives like Peter Jackson sidestepped formal education after the compulsory years. This does not mean that all creative workers have done so, merely that it has been possible for some.

Schooling is still important but for how long? If its irrelevance is now apparent beyond the education industry, then alternative ways and means will be found by enterprising young people to develop the skills, strategies and mental models needed for the 21st-century workplace despite schooling, not because of it. This is of course already happening.

Many commentators like Robinson, and others in the schooling sector, place the blame for locking in Information Age curriculum, pedagogy and assessment on the higher education sector. The argument is that university entrance is a tail wagging a large dog. All those young people who might otherwise want to explore exciting options beyond English, maths and science are unlikely to do so if university entrance scores continue value these test results above all others. When university entrance is the main game, initiatives like student-led media centres are quickly understood to be extracurricular activities, abandoned by 'good' students when the testing pressure is on.

Top-end achievers read the cues about what is valued in the system, whether or not it means engaging with dated concepts. What is tested is what they will pay attention to, so they will funnel their priorities away from multiskilling and towards academic achievement alone. Mark Warschauer cites a study of Chinese immigrant youth in New York who made very clear choices to jettison literacy practices that were not 'directly related to academic success'.[21] When these students are told – as they are in many schools – that twenty-four hours of homework per week is the minimum expected from them in their post-compulsory years, the message is pretty clear that jettisoning extracurricular activities is not just appropriate but mandatory. The message is also clear that the quality of their learning is held to be synonymous with a period of time.

For many young people, the greatest thing about school is that it provides them with a place to meet and interact with their friends. In doing so, they learn the social behaviour that is approved and *verboten* among their particular subgroups. However, adolescents (a category now including anyone from aged from 8 to 30) will not thank anyone who tells them that they are more susceptible to peer pressure than anyone else, a response that any one of us might make to the same accusation.

What they also share, apart from irritation when judged negatively by adults who 'know better', is a preference for interacting through navigator-led, distributed systems that allow them access to each other and to information storage in ways that are unmediated by adults. What schools offer by contrast is overwhelmingly a supply-side, provider-obsessed culture when it comes to the mastery of content and engagement with process. 'We know what is good for you' is the overarching logic of syllabus designers. And couch potato passivity is the understandable behavioural outcome. Student passivity – not bad behaviour – is the biggest obstacle to learning in 21st-century schooling culture.

To redress this problem, we need demand-side thinking focused on learning as a social and networked practice, one that welcomes error at the same time as it celebrates success. Unfortunately there are few signs of this happening in the risk minimisation climate. Indeed, the opposite seems to be true. At the very time when openness and experiment are being widely acknowledged as optimal conditions for

21st-century learning, policy-makers seem to be intent on nailing everything to the floor.

Moral panics don't help

The 'more for less' funding of education globally is very much implicated here. The call is out to all schools to minimise the danger of lower standards, wastage of resources and student failure. Claims that standards are declining, that funds are being wasted, that academic levels are lower than ever – all these are instantly recognisable to teachers and parents alike. Moral panics about literacy, numeracy and the use and abuse of technology are part of a push towards minimising waste and 'raising standards' of traditional literacy, numeracy and the memorising of historical facts.

As a result, we are seeing school and university funding tied to 'outcomes' measured against predetermined government 'standards'. These standards are generally linked to predictable government-approved national priorities such as employability skills and improvements in literacy, numeracy and citizenship. Inevitably these 'skills' are framed with both eyes squarely on an educationally conservative electorate. They both produce and exploit the anxiety that exists in some parts of the public consciousness about a perceived loss of 'cultural foundations'. Under these conditions, 'good spelling' without a spell check and the ability to multiply or divide without calculator take on a moral and civilising purpose. They become much more than skills, despite their decreasing relevance to a digitalised workforce and a global citizenry. It is interesting to note that the lack of capacity to speak a second language – although it might well be regarded as more useful for a globalised workforce – does not seem to evoke the same anxiety in Anglo cultures, as long as the language spoken is, of course, English.

While the air remains thick with calls to innovation, learning opportunities collapse when policy reaffirms the same old skills and disciplines as the things really worth knowing, because they are the only things that are the target of standardised tests. In broad terms, the logic of educational funding has come to fix almost exclusively on performance data that can be standardised in order to allow for intra-state, national and international comparisons. In a performative culture that makes it possible, in theory, to quantify the value of formal education on a national and even global scale, winners can be highly visible and valued, however that calculation is arrived at, while losers can be starved of funding until they get their act together.

It goes without saying that schools in low socioeconomic areas are on a hiding to nothing in this climate.[22] Their slim chance of attracting funding is to frame themselves as special needs schools – again using test data that categorises their student populations as 'high risk' – or their capacity to attract funds from emergent agencies that will provide highly targeted funding to address government-sanctioned social problems, such as obesity, attrition, mental health and so on.

By contrast, schools and universities that have the resources and reputational clout to sit at the top of a league table can give an advantage to students who are similarly aspirational. This means that a significant minority of institutions with the cultural and financial capital to resource their campuses are unlikely to complain about public league tables. Others are much less sanguine. Some critics, for example, argue that what a performative educational culture aspires to is not a high standard of education but 'a high standard of standardness'.[23] Research in the UK, the USA and Australia supports this view,[24] pointing to a trend to value critical, autonomous and creative thinking skills only if and when they can be seen to contribute to productivity as measured by the aggregate examination performance. In simple terms, performance on tests is no longer merely an important instrument or component within the formal education system. It *is* the system.

It does not surprise therefore that, along with the proliferation of league tables and performance indicators, we are now seeing the proliferation of 'excellence' awards, showcase events and other activities associated with identifying and rewarding 'best practice'. Politicians and media commentators alike know the value of selecting and riding themes within the push and pull of the 'bad school/good school' claims. So tales of inefficiency, scandal and systemic failure continue to be made alongside triumphal narratives about an award-winning teacher, an 'against the odds' student or a 'best practice' photo opportunity.

Learning and unlearning are both important

Meanwhile, there is a growing gap between what formal education claims to be doing and what most young people experience on a daily basis in schools. As Mark Warschauer puts it, the challenge of education in this century is to equip young people 'to aim further ahead of a faster target'.[25] Instead, there is growing disquiet about a formal education system that is 'looking in the rear-view mirror',[26] seeking to plan the future by relying on the lessons and habits of the past.

This is deeply flawed logic, according to cultural theorist Zygmunt Bauman.[27] He argues that any useful disposition to learning must map directly on to the 'unfixed' social world and work futures for which young people learn. Bauman evokes the 'rat-in-the-maze' experiments that were the basis of traditional notions of learning to pose hypothetical questions with real implications for this 'liquid' social order:

> What ... if the maze were made of partitions on castors, if the walls changed their position fast, perhaps faster yet than the rats could scurry in search of food, and if the tasty rewards were moved as well, and quickly, and if the targets of the search tended to lose their attraction well before the rats could reach them, while other similarly short-lived allurements diverted their attention and drew away their desire?[28]

This is a metaphor for what has happened to learning, he argues. The capacity to learn and reproduce appropriate social behaviour is no longer the key to success that it once was. Instead of opening up possibilities, much formal learning is actually unhelpful because it assumes a fixed or predictable social world that no longer exits. We train young people in linear–cumulative essay writing while ignoring what counts as good writing for the Internet. We teach the foundations of legal studies despite the fact that they will have almost no relevance to law graduates in their post-degree practice. This means that university students come to acquire the sort of literacies that academics use. As soon as they move away from that setting, they have to jettison or radically rework those same skills for environments in which speed, clarity and breadth of communication matter more than disciplinary jargon and the conventions of formal referencing; that is, they have to unlearn many aspects of these skills because they do not add value outside academe.

In Bauman's 'liquid-modern' social world, the work of assembling and structuring new social relations is no more or less important than the work of keeping them always ready to be dismantled. The focus of learning is moving beyond the individual and the cognitive to incorporate the moral and the aesthetic and the interplay among these various social elements. Put simply, the message we are getting about formal education is 'too much performance, too little learning': too much attention being paid to habits and routines of the Industrial and Information Ages, and too little attention to the skills and capacities that are the working currency of the Conceptual Age.

More creative times ahead?

However, there are now some glimmers of hope in the sea of schooling standardness. In Queensland, educational policy-makers have named the 'Creative Citizen' as one of five 'Overarching Learning Organisers'[29] that make explicit what Queensland state schools value. The attributes they list as marking the Creative Citizen are in keeping with second-generation thinking about the nature of creativity, in their emphasis on creative citizenry as involving a much wider brief than engaging in and valuing of the creative arts:

↪ Understands that creativity is an imaginative and inventive act to produce something new of personal, social and/or cultural value, and can create functional, aesthetic and/or expressive outcomes for self or others using a range of media with technical control.

↪ Understands that innovation is a generative process of identifying problems, building on the ideas and influences of others and producing original solutions, and can recognise patterns and make connections, explore ideas, seize opportunities, challenge conventions and take and manage risk.

↪ Understands that critical self-reflection, making judgments
and acknowledging feedback are an integral part of the creative
process and can take action to refine and modify one's own ideas
and, as creator or consumer, can evaluate and reflect on products
and outcomes.[30]

Where these attributes depart from second-generation thinking is the
extent to which they frame creativity as an individual attribute, ignoring the centrality of co-creation and dynamic team processes.

Yet the fundamental problem remains. The Creative Citizen, as
part of a values framework, is not for assessing. And this, as argued in
chapter 8, will ensure that it remains on the margins of curriculum, not
at its centre.

The Yuk/Wow Generation has the tools to develop a high level
of networking skill that has little to do with their formal education.
They can step around the curriculum and still do the sort of learning
needed to interact with a larger and more challenging world. Through
engagement with and contributions to My Space, Facebook, You Tube
and similar customised, interactive websites, young people can seek out
opportunities and ignore the blockages and obstacles that formal education may put in their way. A recent study of student technology use
at the University of Melbourne found that a significant proportion of
students use emerging computer-based technology such as blogs, file-sharing, social networking, VOIP telephony and web conferencing to
navigate their social and learning pathways.[31] Moreover, students were
'overwhelmingly positive'[32] about the value of information and communications technology (ICT) for their learning. While it does not
necessarily follow that the students want to be taught entirely through
such technology, and while the student population was not uniform in
its access to, use of and levels of proficiency with emerging technology, students are certainly alert to the host of opportunities that digital
tools can provide.

This Australian finding is supported by an OECD study conducted
to find out whether 15-year-old school students were ready for a tech-

nology-rich world.[33] The OECD's PISA study found that, in general, students worldwide are confident in performing routine and Internet tasks on computers, and that Australian students are among the most confident. The study also found that students used their computers for a wide range of purposes, including:

- ↪ looking up information about people, things or ideas on the internet
- ↪ playing games
- ↪ word-processing (with Microsoft Word® or WordPerfect®)
- ↪ collaborating with a group or team via the internet
- ↪ compiling spreadsheets (such as Lotus 1 2 3® or Microsoft Excel®)
- ↪ downloading software (including games) from the internet
- ↪ drawing, painting or otherwise using graphics programs
- ↪ using educational software such as mathematics programs
- ↪ helping to learn school material
- ↪ downloading music from the internet
- ↪ programming to make simple animations and so on
- ↪ communicating electronically (by email or in chat rooms).[34]

These findings refute any notion that playing computer games is *the* singular preoccupation of young people when using computers. This is of particular concern given that so many of their teachers are baby boomers who may be out of touch with the many uses to which computers can be put, beyond finding information and email.

Baby boomer moral panics are not restricted to concerns about 'playing too many computer games'. They also extend to worries about confidentiality and paedophiles lurking on the net. Because Yuk/Wows do not share this moral panic about privacy or confidentiality, as indicated in chapter 1, they often develop and maintain social relationships through their digital technology in a very different way from their grandparents' generation. They will move quickly to test the affordances of digital technology ands virtual neighbourhoods.

All this can sound like quite manic, even dysfunctional, behaviour. Much has been made of 21st-century workers being too driven by fast productivity cycles and the dictum that 'you are only as good as your last month's sales', and with some justification. It's not for those who need a script or a line drawing to keep them from becoming anxious about their job security. However, there is genuine pleasure and richness in achieving what social psychologist Mihaly Csikszentmihalyi calls 'a state of flow',[35] a mental and emotional state in which an individual is simultaneously immersed in and transported by their fixation on an intellectual and/or artistic project. It is a mental and emotional state that certainly can be irritating to those nearby who do not share your passionate compulsion and would rather you 'snapped out of it'. It can even be experienced by those same folk as a form of exclusivity. In some senses, it means that you are not available, not reachable, through habitual social practices like mundane conversation or social niceties. Yet it can be physically exhilarating as an individual experience and can generate a powerful bond among creatives. In a state of flow, individuals can together move faster, fly higher and achieve synergies that are not available to themselves alone. This is more than effective group work, and does not just depend on meeting the right people at the right time. It is dynamic and it is learnable.

Creativity as a group capacity

One of the keys to inducting the Yuk/Wow Generation into the right sort of learning is to help them understand creativity as a characteristic of particular groups, communities or neighbourhoods. While there is no apparent decline of interest in the creative individual, we are at last seeing challenges to the dominant conception of creativity as being fundamentally about personal psychological traits. Pluralising the unit of analysis of creativity raises substantial issues for how we measure creative workforce capacity, in particular our heavy reliance on individual testing to credential young people in schools and universities. If the student cohort or community of learners is the unit to which creative capacity might be more appropriately attributed, then assessment also needs to rely less on individual tests with a sprinkling of group work, and more on demonstrating the thinking and doing of dynamic groups or teams. There is much that needs to change in our mainstream sorting and credentialling processes if we are to provide future employers with credible indicators of the creative capacities of graduates with respect to their demonstrated capability to contribute to high-flying project teams.

We need to be mindful at this point of the concerns expressed by organisational studies expert Amanda Sinclair about the way 'team' is often evoked as the all-purpose solution to organisational success. Sinclair has expressed the view that: '[T]eams are frequently used to camouflage coercion under the pretence of maintaining cohesion; conceal conflict under the guise of consensus; convert conformity into a semblance of creativity; give unilateral decisions a co-determinist seal of approval; delay action in the supposed interests of consultation; legitimize lack of leadership, and disguise expedient arguments and personal agendas.'[36] Put much more simply, there may be no 'I' in team but there remain two 'I's' in 'salary differential'. Appeals to get a 'team-based approach' can have reactionary rather than reformist effects. Moreover, it can level out high-performing individuals who actually might deserve credit for a particular initiative.

If 'team' advocacy has been a special feature of the organisational reform literature, so too the term 'community' has been much loved by progressive educators since the 1980s. Lave and Wenger's scholarship provided a platform for advocating the shift from individualised understanding of learning to emphasising the importance of communities of practice in when and how we learn.[37] With learning framed in more recent times as a social – not simply a cognitive – activity, the value and importance of communities of practice has become a truism of education. Yet we persist in credentialling individuals, not groups or teams or communities.

As is true of the word 'team', the term 'community' is not fresh or innocent. Indeed it has about it the whiff of cheesecloth, evoking a time when 'dropping out' was what communities were for, a far cry from the speeded-up digital environments that characterise the modern organisation. While much lip-service is paid to the need for a sense of community in the new workplace culture, CEOs and senior managers are usually absent from the seminars given on this topic by enthusiastic members of the human resources department.

The terms 'neighbourhood' and 'flockmates' borrowed from computer animations of natural systems – swarming and flocking – seem to come with less baggage attached. 'Flocking' behaviour, as in computer simulations of 'boids' (bird objects) works from a set of behavioural principles that allow flocks or swarms to perform with greater capacity (such as moving higher and faster and avoiding obstacles more adeptly) than the capacity of any one flock member.[38] The relevance of this to the creative workforce is elaborated in chapter 7.

So what?

Creative capacity needs high levels of literacy, both traditional and digital. Many of the digital skills and interpersonal capacities students need are not acquired in formal education. This means that schools and universities are increasingly irrelevant to the creative workforce. Schools and universities will continue to be irrelevant to the creative futures of young people if the culture of teaching and learning within them treats students as passive consumers of predetermined information rather than active co-creators of knowledge.

Yet it will not be enough to be digitally savvy. Young people who work as creatives will have to be proficient in both learning and unlearning. This is because the 'correct' formula or routine for solving a particular problem today cannot be relied on to fix a similar problem tomorrow. Some pioneering work is being done to make formal education more relevant, but it is very little and very late.

The big building blocks of the command and control culture of the last two centuries remain relatively intact. So the job of putting creativity at the centre of curriculum, pedagogy and assessment in schools and universities is a daunting one. We cannot rely on the identification of a few examples of innovative and exciting educational practice to join the dots of creative endeavour and by that means transform our creaking organisational systems. And we cannot rely on custodial institutions to throw caution to the winds in the service of experiment and innovation.

There are things we can do as knowing users of, and practitioners within, our education systems. First, we need to acknowledge that:

- ↳ 'unlearning' and 'useful ignorance' will be more valuable than sure knowing
- ↳ participative, interactive, team-oriented activity will be more useful than recall
- ↳ open (including technology-enhanced) environments will be more useful than closed environments
- ↳ uncertainty and fluidity will be more useful than surety and dumbing down
- ↳ coping with complexity will be better done through simple rules and clear goals than through complex rules and systemic arrangements.

Four key implications flow from this for the orientation of educators to their work. The work must shift:

- ↳ from delivering content to building capacity
- ↳ from supply and demand chains to value-added networks
- ↳ from setting curriculum to creating curriculum
- ↳ from a focus on books to a focus on the screens and from desktop technology to hand-held or mobile learning technology.

New new basics?

The sort of content that seems much more relevant to lifestyle, learning and earning could include such interesting new areas as:

- ↳ portfolio career management
- ↳ project management and entrepreneurship
- ↳ techno-literacy
- ↳ project-based work in teams

- international engagement
- life design (how to make strategic decisions about your future)
- capacity to navigate from entry-level jobs to wealth-creating destinations
- learning to learn (or how to be a self-managing learner).

The following list sets out the things to which we should be committing ourselves or discontinuing, if learning is to be relevant to living 'over the horizon'.

- IN: 'unlearning' and 'useful ignorance'
- OUT: sure knowing
- IN: participative, interactive, team-oriented activity
- OUT: recalling content
- IN: open (including technology-enhanced) environments
- OUT: closed environments
- IN: uncertainty and fluidity
- OUT: surety and dumbing down
- IN: coping with complexity through simple rules and clear goals
- OUT: complex rules and systemic arrangements.

Some of the most promising of these concepts are presented in the chapters that follow.

Teacher: sage, guide, meddler

Teachers matter. They matter because of the lasting impression they give to their students about whether or not learning is a pleasant or useful thing to do. Some teachers can't resist being a 'Sage-on-the-Stage', despite the now decades-old advocacy of 'Guide-on-the-Side' as the more enlightened role. Whatever they do or fail to do, teachers have a powerful influence in turning young people on or off learning. This chapter sets out a case for moving beyond the binary formulation of teachers as either 'Sage-on-the-Stage' or 'Guide-on-the-Side', to a third role for the 21st-century teacher as a builder of creative capacity – that of Meddler-in-the-Middle.

The Sage-or-Guide binary is very familiar to teachers. It is used to differentiate teaching styles or teaching moments as either teacher-centred or student-centred. The following excerpt from Jamie Mackenzie's 'Wired Classroom' exemplifies the familiarity of this binary formulation in literature about teaching.

A good teacher knows when to act as Sage on the Stage and when to act as a Guide on the Side. Because student-centred learning can be time-consuming and messy, efficiency will sometimes argue for the Sage. When students are busy making up their own minds, the role of the teacher shifts. When questioning, problem-solving and investigation become the priority classroom activities, the teacher becomes a Guide on the Side.[1]

What is implied here is that all teaching activity is subsumed under one category or the other. As the writer himself understands it, 'Guide-on-the-Side' covers a vast and daunting panoply of activities: 'circulating, redirecting, disciplining, questioning, assessing, guiding, directing, fascinating, validating, facilitating, moving, monitoring, challenging, motivating, watching, moderating, diagnosing, trouble-shooting, observing, encouraging, suggesting, watching, modelling and clarifying.'[2]

The difficulty here is that 'guiding' or 'facilitating' rarely involves all these things. Many of the teachers who see themselves as 'guide' are as unlikely to be 'fascinating' as they are to be 'challenging'. In reality, we have seen the high ground of 'guiding' too easily collapse into passive childminding and worksheet distribution. 'Guide-on-the-Side' then becomes a high moral–ethical excuse for the teacher to step out of the main game of teaching and to sit at the margins of the physical, mental and emotional activity that is so vital to learning. And when the teacher sits down, figuratively speaking, the students lie down.

Both the 'Sage-on-the Stage' and 'Guide-on-the-Side' have their place in the complex landscape that is teaching. The point is that stepping down from the podium in order to hand out worksheets, or simply hoping that students are 'on task' at computer terminals or watching a DVD, is no solution to the pedagogical challenges of teaching for the twenty-first century. The enemy of 21st-century learning is not student disobedience, nor is it low literacy levels – it is passivity.

'Sages-on-the-Stage' need student passivity in order to be the centre of the action (rightfully, of course!). So the measure of the effective 'Sage' is one who has a quiet classroom focused on listening and following instructions. 'Guides-on-the-Side' reject this positioning of themselves. Guides focus on their students, preparing tasks for them in advance of the class, ensuring that they are clear about the nature of the task, then they move quietly and supportively around the room, one of many 'learning objects' in the environment.

The risk is that the teacher too is now pretty passive, and the message this gives is that learning is unremarkable. It passes the time – time that, as Samuel Beckett reminds us, would have passed anyway. In replacing the disciplinary straitjacket and terror of the tyrant's cane with the worksheet and the whispering voice of the counsellor, we congratulate ourselves on taking the tyranny out of our teaching. Yet the worksheet is as unlikely as the cane to meet the challenges of 21st-century learning, whatever its achievements in 'keeping their heads down'. An invitation to 'colour in the Roman helmet at the bottom of the page when you've finished answering the questions' is no substitute for rigorous and exciting learning.

Meddler-in-the Middle is a much more active and interventionist role. It positions the teacher and student as mutually involved in assembling and disassembling cultural products. The teacher is in there doing and making mistakes alongside students, not just moving like Florence Nightingale from desk to desk or chat room to chat room, watching, encouraging and monitoring. Meddling is a re-positioning of teacher and student as co-directors and co-editors of their social world. As a learning partnership, meddling has powerful implications for what 'content' is considered worthy of engagement, how the value of the learning product is to be assessed and who the rightful assessor is to be.

Meddler-in-the-Middle challenges longer-term notions of 'good' teaching in a number of ways. Specifically, it means:

↪ less time giving instructions and more time spent being a usefully ignorant team member in the thick of the action
↪ less time spent being a custodial risk minimiser and more time spent being an experimenter, risk-taker and learner
↪ less time spent being a forensic classroom auditor and more time spent being a designer, editor and assembler
↪ less time spent being a counsellor and 'best buddy' and more time spent being a collaborative critic and authentic evaluator.

These priorities are not easily achieved because of the weight of past teaching practice and the inflexibility of formal education systems. In what follows, the role of the classroom teacher is put under scrutiny. The intention is to understand the significance of the legacy of teaching cultures; that is, the significance of what we have inherited as sanctioned modes of working on, with or for students. Without this, any advocacy for changing hard-wired systemic practices is a naive hope at best. The new assemblage of roles and identities needed when teaching for creativity will inevitably have to stand on the shoulders of past practice, at least to some extent. This will both enable and constrain what it is possible for teachers to think and do in their daily pedagogical work.

Teachers will wreck any plan for reform, if they do not see it as achievable in practical terms or if they do not see its value in moral and ethical terms. This is both a strength and a limitation. Individuals do not usually join the profession to get rich, and if they did they would be sorely disappointed. They are not looking to self-promote or to sell products. They are a sceptical lot, who are conservative as a whole, and remain highly suspicious of the Next Big Thing that is coming to reform and restructure them.

This means that any romantic call to greater creativity that does not take the conditions of teaching and the sensibilities of the teacher into account is bound to fail. What follows is an insider's attempt to locate and name the 'wiggle room' in cultures of teaching, rather than to incite revolution by colonising education with business models, or insisting on some free-floating manifesto that will 'save' 21st-century children. There is always wiggle room, even in the most rigid of systems, and there is always constraint, even in what is apparently the most open of invitations.

'Every eye on me'

The leaders of the past – like the Sage-on-the-Stage – knew very well the importance of attracting and maintaining the gaze of those who surrounded them. A great teacher had no rival in the classroom. He was elevated above those around him, god-like in terms of the aura surrounding him and the power he wielded. His word was sacrosanct and his authority unquestioned. Of course, not all teachers who aspired to this status were able to achieve it. I once worked for a school principal with many with god-like aspirations who was notorious for his furious response to a parent who accused him of being a petty tyrant. 'A tyrant I don't mind', he said, 'but a *petty* tyrant?!'

God-like aspirations notwithstanding, it is a long time since the word 'great' has been used to describe teachers with any conviction. Once used so freely as a descriptor of famous individual teachers – Socrates, Mohammed, the Buddha, Jesus – 'great' is now tainted in educational scholarship and teacher professionalism literature. It is tainted by the implication that greatness demands pedagogical authority and discipleship, a demand that we are all supposed to have eschewed a long time ago. Any invitation to discipleship, apprenticeship or other vertical model of instruction-led pedagogy is suspect for its reliance on the ability of One Great Man to attract others to him by the sheer power of his personality and his authority.

Yet the ghost of the Great Man still haunts formal education. While it has been thoroughly expelled from early childhood education (where there are as few aspirations to 'greatness' as there are men to teach), it becomes a palpable presence in the post-compulsory sector. When teaching disciplines takes priority over teaching people, the temptation to perform as a god-like figure is irresistible to many. In contexts like universities where academics have been rewarded for what they know, and the claims they can make to international recognition for the 'quality' and impact of their intellectual output, it is understandable, if regrettable, that this is so.

Why is the Teacher-as-Authority-Figure becoming more irrelevant to 21st-century education? And, in particular, why are they increasingly irrelevant to creative capacity-building? One way to investigate both the seduction and the problem of teacher-as-god is through scrutinising the difference between popular artists of the 20th century, like Freddie Mercury of Queen and the popular 21st-century ensemble Blue Man Group. Both are talented, charismatic and creative. Both are attuned to the culture of their times. The difference is that Freddie was then and Blue Man Group is now. This is not to say that other members of Queen were not important too. The 'pop' group was all the rage thirty years ago. But it was always important to be able to identify each member as a separate and individual 'talent' within the group identity. Blue Man Group does not make such distinctions. There is no 'frontman' so there is no single entity that is the main focus of attention.

Freddie Mercury's performance at the 1985 Live-Aid Concert is legendary. As was true of all Mercury's on-stage performances, it was highly dependent on his singular capacity to 'tease, shock and ultimately charm his audience with various extravagant versions of himself'.[3] His capacity to mesmerise an audience of 72,000 people at the Wembley Stadium concert was a tribute to his ability to keep every eye on him.

Freddie Mercury exploited every theatrical ploy, but he went further than others had done before him when it same to invoking audience participation. He did not separate himself from 'ordinary' others; instead, he drew on his audience to be part of the performance in ways that were unprecedented at the time, anticipating to some extent at least the interactivity that would be the strong preference of the post-millennial audiences he would not live to entertain. Nevertheless, the essence of Mercury's pedagogy was the embodied individual, Freddie – singular, charismatic, theatrical, god-like. He directed all the pedagogical traffic, and that was how everyone liked it in the 1980s.

Compare this with Blue Man Group three decades later. Described as a 'creative organisation' rather than a band,[4] Blue Man Group applies a unique process of creating and performing to a wide variety of projects, including concerts, film and TV scoring, commercial campaigns and museum exhibits. Moreover, they appeal to a wide range of age groups and cultural backgrounds.

While Mercury's performances were focused on one man to the exclusion of all else, Blue Man Group has three 'frontmen'. There is no singular focus. The three frontmen are undifferentiated in terms how they look or what they do. All three have blue plasticised faces and grey 'pyjama-style' costumes, and all play a variety of percussion instruments, including the underside of an upturned piano and constantly readjusted configurations of PVC pipes.

The frontmen work together to deliver a performance in which no individual performer dominates. Throughout the performance, the three nameless and voiceless frontmen react, in a parody of childlike bewilderment, to (adult) commands from a voice-over announcer who is never seen, working both with and against the authoritative voice, and encouraging the audience to do likewise.

At times, the three blue men are displaced by simulacra, but with no loss of esteem for the performing body – simulacrum and flesh have parity in the performance. Their playful substitution of image for flesh parallels Nintendo's invitation to its Mii customers to create caricatured portraits of themselves that fit a preferred personality for use in compatible Wii video games.[5] The invitation is to pluralise singular identities through customisation – and, through that affordance, to have fun. While the physical body is always eventually disappointing in what it can achieve, the identities it is possible to create do not have such limitations. They can jump higher, run faster, hit harder than anyone – including the world's best. Why privilege the physical when the simulacrum is the source of so much capability and pleasure?

Much of the performative excitement of Blue Man Group is generated through stunts and special effects that are designed to engage most of the senses most of the time. One stunt is noteworthy for overturning the norms of pedagogical engagement by turning the audience gaze on itself. This is achieved when the 'frontmen' enter the audience with cameras to probe – literally – the inner workings of the biological bodies of individual audience members. These 'gullet' images are simultaneously made accessible on the big screen, mocking the forensic gaze of the audience, while at the same time being self-mocking, an invitation to fun and parody.

Blue Man Group concerts, needless to say, are more than busy – indeed, they are relentless in terms of activity, with multiple things going on at any one time and multiple identities performing, including the audience. This is a deliberate strategy conceived by the Blue Man 'captain', Anthony Parrulli. His rationale for generating the multiplicity of unusual sights and sounds that mark the performance of Blue Man Group is very much one of refusing the passivity that was an audience's lot at a rock concert or sporting event in previous times. Parrulli is quoted as saying, 'I always wanted to take [a rock concert] apart … I didn't want to watch. I wanted to play.'[6]

The playfulness of Blue Man Group has invaded not only the world of the rock concert but also an educational world desperately in need of an infusion of 'hands-on' excitement. Their 1500-square-foot travelling exhibit invites patrons to make their own music on PVC pipes, Slide-u-Lums (a blend of drum and slide trombone), Build-u-Lums (a form of Lego using pipes of different lengths), a Surround Sound Theatre and so on. Throughout their engagement with the exhibits, visitors are invited to use their bodies, not simply drag them around as passive carcasses. Their enthusiasm for engagement is childlike in the best sense. As group member Lou Quintanilla puts it: 'In a lot of ways, the Blue Man is like a child; he'll look at the world in a different light that adults would see as mundane and turn it into something new and musical … Blue Man is big on new ways of learning and entertaining that teaches kids how to think on that level and not just rely on what is taught.'[7]

In drawing on the forms and the formats used by young people to learn and be entertained, but integrating these into the wide array of their performative activities, Blue Man Group brings the Nintendo generation's preference for interactivity and playfulness to their mode of audience engagement. No single adult is the focus of attention, nor is anyone expected to remain out of the action. While Freddie Mercury pre-empted audience participation, Blue Man Group take participation and interactivity into another dimension, aided and abetted by the affordances of smart communication technology.

The 'hands on, minds on, plugged in' form of entertainment that characterises Blue Man Group provides a host of clues for 21st-century teachers seeking first to engage a new generation of young people, then prepare them for the creative workforce. In particular, they show the importance of 'identity-forming activity' for enculturation into a field of practice, what educationist John Seely Brown calls 'learning to be' rather than 'learning about'.[8] Audience members are explicitly invited to reject the passive role of onlookers, in the same way that visitors to their exhibits are invited to reject the role of merely 'passing through'. Through participating actively, the audience becomes part of the community of entertainers, 'prod-users'[9] of fun and entertainment, not just passive consumers of externally produced 'products'.

It is not simply that passivity becomes increasingly impossible in the context, but that the modes of engagement invite the audience to join in the playful activity that is the essence of the persona of Blue Man Group. In so doing, the group invites Seely Brown's 'peripheral participation' as an antecedent to entering a community of practice. 'In peripheral participation the student is engaged in real work ... He or she is able ... to pick up, as though through osmosis, the sensibilities, beliefs, and idiosyncrasies of the particular community of practice. Learning happens seamlessly as part of an enculturation process as the learner moves from the periphery to a more central position in the community.'[10] The disposition to fun and play through music-making is an important antecedent to more meaningful engagement through more rigorous thinking and doing. It does not guarantee value-added creativity of the quality of Blue Man Group, but the invitation is an explicit entrée into a world in which one can 'be musical', as distinct from merely watching musicality being performed 'from the outside'.

As elaborated in the previous chapter, formal education has a lot of difficulty finding a place for fun after the infant grades. However, young people do not. Marc Prensky writes of the extent to which college students can and do prioritise fun over mandated activity:[11] 'One college student recently confided to me that he had skipped an exam because he was so close to "beating" a video game.' He concludes that 'the true 21st-century learning revolution is finally throwing off the shackles of pain and suffering that have accompanied it for so long' and that in our own lifetimes we will see learning become 'infinitely more learner-centred and fun' for all of education's stakeholders.[12]

Learning might well be fun, but we cannot depend on formal education to adopt this idea any time soon. Indeed, with all the moral panics around declining literacy levels of students, drugs in schools and lack of discipline in schools, Prensky's vision seems some way off for institutional education. Moreover, we should not underestimate students' own grudging acceptance that schools are meant to be tedious and boring. Students can be the most powerful force for conservatism once they have been enculturated into schooling as passive consumption. My experience of many well-schooled senior students on a hot Friday afternoon is that they are more than likely to cut across the 'activity' plans of excited student teachers by responding: 'Just give us the ten main points – we don't want to do any experiments or experiential drama. Our fun happens outside school!'

Being scientific

The disposition to creativity – that is, to the discipline and pleasure of moving ideas from one state to another – demands that young people unlearn such passivity and learn through active engagement. Creativity is not something that is genetically programmed or bought at the shop. It can and should be learned. And one way to begin this process is to make explicit the difference between 'learning about' and 'learning to be'. Teachers have not, as a profession, been very successful at either understanding this difference or communicating it to their students. Benjamin Franklin once said: 'Tell me and I forget, teach me and I remember, involve me and I learn.'[13] Traditional teaching has been concerned with the first two of these forms of exchange, but paid much less attention to the third.

The teaching of science is a case in point. The failure of our science teachers to induct young people into the scientific community – into thinking like a scientist – has precipitated much hand-wringing in university faculties of science. If the goal of science teachers is to 'expose [students] to the discovery process and to excite them about challenges at the frontiers of science', then science faculties have a big problem, argues science educator Bruce Alberts.[14] Not only are fewer students opting for undergraduate science degrees to discover and be excited by science but also fewer students are remaining to complete their degrees for the same reason.

The failure of science teaching to induct a new generation into scientific thinking is not a sudden or dramatic discovery. Indeed, the clock has been ticking on conventional science pedagogy for a long time.[15] Yet there is little evidence of pedagogical shift in science despite all the evidence that the flight from science is real and damaging to economic and social endeavour, and that the way science is taught makes it frightening to many young people who are otherwise fascinated by the world around them. The significant downturn in students choosing the enabling sciences is a global problem in the developed world, where there is a very real risk of losing a generation of science graduates skilled in the core disciplines. Yet science teaching remains incredibly hard-wired and resistant to change.

So what are we dealing with here? For a community so driven by evidence, how can we explain the stubborn resistance of teachers to make the shift from 'learning about' to 'learning to be' against all the evidence?

A number of explanations could be given. One is that most teachers teach in the same way they were taught. If, as is likely, the majority of science teachers still hail from a baby boomer generation that learned its science through 'Sage-on-the-stage' instruction, then this will continue to be the dominant pedagogical model. Most students will 'experience' science as an endless stream of increasingly complex information being delivered by a singular teacher or lecturer in classrooms and/or lecture halls.

In such a top-down pedagogical relationship, invitations to 'be scientific' are constrained by concerns that students will not have enough information to do the rigorous experimenting, analytic thinking and calculation needed by scientists in their daily practice. Students in the junior school are told that they need 'the basics' before they can begin to think like scientists. 'Being scientific' will have to wait for the post-compulsory years, by which time most will have deserted science. Those who do enrol in science in the senior years of high school are likely to be told early and often that they have an information deficit

The creative workforce

that must be treated before they can hope for more. The pleasure and rigour of 'being scientific' will have to wait until they go to university. University lecturers, of course, will be appalled by what these students don't know in first-year chemistry or physics, and will insist that 'foundations' need to be laid before any 'higher-order' work can be done. And so deferral of induction – with all its rigour and its pleasure – is always defensible, as well as endless.

It is not a matter of blaming or shaming. Few science teachers have anything but the best of intentions. They are genuinely concerned about the learning deficits of their students and genuinely determined to overcome them in order to provide a platform of information on which higher-order scientific knowledge might one day be built. What they are doing, however, is ensuring that science students remain outside the scientific community and its creative practices. Selecting, reshuffling, combining or synthesising existing facts, ideas and skills in original ways – these are things leading scientists do every day to address global problems and find solutions. To move forward they rely on creativity, not just the routines of their inquiry.

Scientists certainly do need information. However, they do not need information overload, nor do they need to memorise large quantities of information. Indeed, this can be downright dangerous, given the limited shelf-life of so many of our scientific 'facts'. According to Seely Brown, the conditions that are more likely to induct students into 'being scientific' are, by contrast, those that combine 'the power of passion-based participation in niche communities of [scientific] practice' with a 'limited core curriculum',[16] not a curriculum that expands exponentially in terms of the quantity of information for memorising and regurgitating. Where large quantities of information are taken as the marker of disciplinary rigour, then opportunities for induction into a professional field are put in jeopardy.

Choosing useful ignorance

Why persist, then, with so much information 'about' science or any other disciplinary field (law, accounting, architecture)? Finally, it is not a question of rationality but of emotion. Yet the importance of 'irrationality' to learning and engagement is not acknowledged, much less rewarded, in formal educational contexts.

To invite teachers to move outside their pedagogical comfort zones – that is, as suppliers of information to an insufficiently informed student body – is to invite them to turn from the very things for which they have been rewarded in the past. It is also to invite scrutiny of their present in terms of the extent to which they themselves are authentically integrated into a community of practice beyond the teaching community. All this as well as having to confront the need to learn much that is new. So opting for the discomfort of doing different pedagogical work would be an irrational choice on a number of levels. Fear of emptying out the curriculum, fear of fads and fashions as superficial and dumbed down, fear of not knowing what to do, fear of losing the status of 'authority'. These fears are real, and they are not easily overturned by calls to begin the next pedagogical revolution.

It is worth remembering how unpopular eminent psychologist Carl Rogers was in his own community of practice at Columbia University for his 'revolutionary educational thinking'. In the early 1950s, Rogers insisted that formal education erred in focusing on the personality of the teacher when it was the learner who ought to be the centre and focus of pedagogy. 'I have come to feel', said Rogers, 'that the only learning that significantly influences behaviour is self-discovered, self-appropriated learning ... I realise that I have lost interest in being a teacher.'[17] It is understandable that his colleagues who were busy training 'Sage-on-the-Stage' teachers would indeed be confronted by this *volte face* in attending to the learner, not the teacher.

More confronting still for teachers and those who train them is to be put in a situation of not knowing, when one of the most deeply held assumptions of contemporary teachers is that they ought to know more about their subject matter than their students. Since the days of Peter Abelard, there has been a heavy social investment in the idea that teachers deliver wisdom to students who sit – either physically or metaphorically – at the feet of the wise one. Whether or not we view a good teacher as the Sage-on-the-Stage or the Guide-on-the-Side (or a bit of both), teachers are still generally expected – and expect themselves – to earn their keep by being 'ahead' of their students in terms of their overall knowledge and understanding.

British journalist and social commentator Charlie Leadbeater challenges the myth that lurks behind habitual thinking about the teacher as knower; that is, the myth that we are becoming a more and more knowledgeable society with each new generation.[18] If knowing means being intimately familiar with the workings of the technology we use in our daily lives, then, Leadbeater asserts, we have never been more ignorant. He reminds us that our great-grandparents had an intimate knowledge of the technology around them, and had no problem with getting the butter churn to work or preventing the lamp from smoking. Few of us would know what to do if our mobile phones stopped functioning, just as few have familiarity with what is underneath or behind the keys on our computers. Nor, indeed, do many of us want to. But this means that we are all very quickly reduced to the quill and the lamp if we lose our power sources or our machines break down. This makes us much more vulnerable – as well as much more ignorant in relative terms – than our predecessors. Put another way, the gap between the knowledge embedded in our everyday environment and what we individually know is greater than ever.

Leadbeater makes a further important point that turns our assumptions about the usefulness of knowledge itself on its head. It is not simply that we are ignorant about the knowledge embedded in the technology we use; it is that we need to put this ignorance to work – to make it useful – to provide opportunities for ourselves and others to live innovative and creative lives, because, as Leadbeater puts it, 'What holds people back from taking risks is often as not ... their knowledge, not their ignorance.'[19] Useful ignorance, then, is a space of pedagogical possibility, not a gap. 'Not knowing' can be put to work without shame or bluster.

This sort of thinking has its parallels in Guy Claxton's notion of 'resilient learning' as 'knowing what to do when you don't know what to do'.[20] Claxton makes the point that our highest educational achievers may well be aligned with their teachers in knowing what to do only if and when they have the script. However, this sort of certain knowing does not work in the script-less and fluid social world in which we live. Our best teachers will be those who understand how to make 'not knowing' useful, who can throw away the blueprint, the template, the map, and help their students make a new kind of sense.

Below are two instances of such teaching. The examples describe how two teachers, well known to me from my teaching experience, have put 'meddling' pedagogy principles into action, the former in a high school English class and the latter in a high school science class. They demonstrate the point that the expertise needed to engage young people in productive and creative endeavour is not predicated on having more or better technology. Nor is it predicated on a strong record of academic success on the part of the students being taught. In the first exemplar, the students are working-class boys in a large Catholic secondary college, and they have a full range of test results, from very high achievement to very limited achievement. In the second, the students are long-term failures and disrupters of science in a large junior secondary state school class.

Example 5.1 Meddling with Macbeth

Teaching *Macbeth* was not going to work if I had to force-feed these kids on it. I didn't want to throw Shakespeare out of the curriculum, and I wasn't going to drag them through it – y'know, 'I know it's painful but it's good for you!'

I began with nothing in their hands or mine – no books, no pens, no notes, no Shakespeare. 'OK', I said, 'a king has been murdered. You are detectives, and you have to solve the murder. That means you have to come up with the means, the motive and the opportunity. You can interview anyone who was at the castle with two exceptions. You can't interview the king's sons because they went off on horses during the night, and you can't interview the three old women who were hanging around last night because they have disappeared. Of course, the ones you can interview might tell you lies, but you are detectives and your job is to see through all that.'

I divided them into about six or seven rival detective agencies, each having to come up with their version of what happened. I gave them a list of names of who they could interview, and I went into whichever role asked. If they wanted to speak to Lady Macbeth, I took that on; if they wanted to speak to the porter I did that, too.

Now the crime of killing Duncan, and the cover-up, are quite complex, as you would probably know. It involves a number of incidents and more than one individual, not just Macbeth. So coming up with Means, Motive and Opportunity is quite complicated. They listened, got together to theorise, and then asked some more.

I let them try out their ideas when they thought they had it. I would not make it easy for them. Of course they wanted to know what actually happened pretty well straight away, but I was not letting them off the hook of the work of theorising. And I wanted them to do it together – to value each other's smarts, not just mine. I acknowledged it when they were moving in the right direction but would not give more – they struggled for every inch of the truth and it had to be right. They continued to ask to interview characters and I continued to play the parts.

I knew I was getting what I wanted – their engagement with Shakespeare – when I saw a few boys trying to sneak a peek at the textbook under the desk. This was great – although I feigned annoyance that they were not on task.

Eventually, after few lessons, we got there. They had it all – and were pretty pleased about it to boot!

After that, we moved on to riddles. 'If Macbeth will never lose his crown until the woods move to the castle, then what does this mean? If no man born of women shall harm Macbeth, then how might he die?' And so on. They took a few wrong turns, and it was important that they should. Yep, Macbeth might be killed by a child, but this does not happen. Yep, Macbeth might fall over a cliff accidentally, but this doesn't happen either.

But once they'd cracked the murder and the riddles, they had the play. What is most significant, I think, is that after this, none of the boys appeared to struggle in any really negative way with Shakespearean prose – they enjoyed it all thoroughly. They were proud of themselves for learning so much about something they presumed was 'way above' them – at least, this is what their parents and older siblings had told them: Shakespeare sucks and it's hard. I've seen teachers throw out these opportunities because they think the boys won't be able to cope. The fact is that they will if you give them access. That's the job of the teacher in my book – giving access, not dumbing down!

Macbeth is great play for adolescent boys. I could have put the DVD of Polanski's *Macbeth* on right at the start, and they would have immediate access, but this is too easy and too much is lost. The opportunity to struggle for it is just not there. Later, when the learning had happened through their deep and close engagement with the what, how and why, yes, then they watched the DVD – and yes, then they did enjoy the lovely young Lady Macbeth in a state of undress!

A number of student teachers came in to watch these lessons. Later they said to me, 'It's terrific watching you do it, but we couldn't do it – we don't know the play well enough.'

Example 5.2 Meddling with motors

They were year 9 students who had a reputation for disrupting every science lesson for one entire semester. As head of the science department, I knew that the morale of my teaching staff was being sapped, and there was every likelihood that next semester would be the same story. So before the start of semester 2, I told them: 'I will take them all out of your classes so you can get on with your teaching. They will be my class.'

While that solved a problem for the other teachers, it gave me eighteen big ones – a class of 14-year-old boys and girls who had failed science and who knew how to bring any science lesson to a halt. On the first day of the new term, I made my decision not to teach them. I said, 'I won't try to teach you science – you have shown that you don't want to learn science and that this would be a lost cause. You can disrupt any class and you will disrupt mine – you'll beat me every time so I won't teach you science.'

They were not sure about this – my job was to be their victim and I wouldn't do it. 'So what are we gonna do for science class?'

'There's a choice', I said, 'we can do nothing or we can have a go at doing some stuff that is not in the curriculum but you might find interesting to do.' They opted for the latter choice, although they were by no means won over that this stage.

As a disadvantaged school, our school had been the 'beneficiary' of second-hand resources that were the rejects from other schools. This included about a dozen motor kits that were shoved in the back of a cupboard in the prep room.

I got the eighteen kids into six groups of three (they self-selected into these groups – I know from past experience if you try to set up groups to avoid putting the worst with the worst you are bound to get it wrong!) and gave each group a kit to assemble. None of the kits came with instructions, and they got few from me. My intention was they might learn by co-operating with each other rather disrupting each other or competing with me.

For want of anything better to do in some respects they began to try assembling the bits and pieces to get a motor that worked. My job was to put them in touch with each other's efforts, not tell them what to do. In fact there were kids in that class who knew a bloody sight more than me about motors – they'd been working on cars all their lives. When one group seemed to be getting a move along, I told them to speak to a group that was slightly ahead in terms of progress. I wanted to acknowledge their efforts – stickability and success and listening respectfully to their peers were all new to them – but it was just as important that they begin to respect the efforts and capability of their peers.

When it came time to see who had the motor that functioned best, the groups whose constructions did so were not the ones that I would have predicted. The kids who had pushed on further, experimenting with more possibilities for customisation, had lost some of their firepower in the process. However, they had been sufficiently acknowledged as the 'progressives' that by now they did not need to win any contest.

During this time, a few individuals began to ask me if they as a class could be taught science. I did not immediately accede to this, surprised and pleased though I was. I needed proof that the whole class was prepared to participate, not just the few enthusiasts who approached me. When this was forthcoming, within the first three weeks of the new semester, we had a contract to have a 'real' science class. By the time the semester finishes, only two of the class had remained at the same level of low achievement they began with. All the others had improved, some quite dramatically.

I think the point is that I would not work against them nor would I let them work against me. It was not a cop-out – just an acknowledgment that these kids would not engage with the same old science. Something had to change if there was any chance of re-engagement, and that was my job. Because if they're not engaged, you're dead in the water.

These two teachers have much in common. They do not let students 'off the hook' of challenge, neither do they kid themselves about the difference between teaching and child-minding. They have clear intentions about what they do, and they are energetically up and doing. 'Command and control' is not the ethos that drives their actions, nor is their teaching by any means *laissez-faire*. They provide support and direction through structure-rich activity in which they themselves are highly involved. They do not take over the work of thinking and doing, nor do they dumb things down. In these ways they demonstrate what 'meddling' pedagogical expertise looks like as daily classroom practice.

Teaching as creative capacity-building

What, then, is it that makes these useful exemplars of teaching as creative capacity-building? It could well be argued that they are simply examples of good teaching and that we could find such examples anywhere.

Let's look more closely at what is going on here. First, these teaching incidents are uncommon, despite the fact that they could be a daily occurrence in schools. The fact that the other science teachers were not able to have any influence on the learning of 'disruptive' kids over an entire semester, the fact that student teachers felt they could not emulate this introduction to Shakespeare, much as they admired it – these things indicate that such teaching is not mainstream practice, nor can we expect it to be any time soon.

It is more common, unfortunately, for teachers to give up on disruptive kids (who are most likely to be among the most disadvantaged kids), to abandon Shakespeare in favour of more popular reading or to play a film or provide comprehension tasks or notes, rather than to engage in rigorous problem-solving when it comes to Shakespearean plots or motor mechanics.

What is clear is from these anecdotes is how well aligned this teaching is with the principles of creative organisational leadership, as elaborated at the end of the previous chapter. First, they demonstrate the technical expertise of an experienced and capable teacher-as-leader. Next, they put into practice strategies that require both themselves and their students to stay in the zone of 'sense-making and joint problem-solving'.[21] The emphasis is on working in teams towards a specific end which the teacher/leader has clearly in mind; that is, these teachers can envisage the 'downstream consequences of successful implementation'[22] of their pedagogy.

They do not underestimate the difficulties of moving students from a negative disposition to a particular disciplinary domain to a positive one. Just as effective leaders of creative effort understand that 'creative efforts are difficult and demanding ventures that involve stress and conflict', so too these teachers – and their students – might have had an easier life if they cut back on 'challenging missions'[23] in the classroom and handed out 'keep 'em busy' worksheets, which is easier but much less effective in terms of helping them to experience learning as a pleasant and useful thing to do.

While not using routine work to 'anchor' students, these teachers are well aware of the importance of maintaining a focus on the task at hand and ensure that the students are similarly focused. In this sense, they are quite different from Blue Man Group, whose 'pedagogy' involves having multiple things going on at any time. But then a teacher's job is to develop the students' capacity to learn. To develop their high level of skill, each member of Blue Man Group would likewise have to focus for many hours on the craft he now employs to entertain their audiences. The discipline of maintaining focus is not easily developed in a world in which there is constant interruption. Again, technology may be more of a hindrance than a help in doing so.

To do the tough work of dispositional change – that is, to have students change their habits away from short-term gains and fear of rigour – requires a high level of social skill on the part of these teachers. For example, the invitation to disruptive students to choose between doing nothing and doing something could easily have come unstuck if it were not handled skilfully. These teachers, like leaders of creative efforts, are 'fast on their feet'[24] – they are flexible without being easily 'bought'. They respond with appropriate pedagogical skill to any attempt to circumvent the rigorous process of thinking and theorising, refusing to pander to the students. At the same time, they appear to enjoy interacting with them once the rules have been established and are being followed.

A teacher's enjoyment of their students simply cannot be faked – students always see through such contrived displays as patronising. This is a point that 'Guide-on-the-Side' models tend to underrate: the importance of the evidence of a teacher's pleasure in the learning of their students. We have been very suspicious of teacher pleasure for a long time for a range of historical reasons to do with how much teacher pleasure has been had at the expense of students.[25] However, it is time to restore teacher pleasure as one of the markers of teaching for creativity. Without knowing that a teacher takes great pleasure in the problem-solving work of their students, there are no cues that (a) the work is pleasurable in itself or (b) the teacher actually cares one way or the other. When the reward is simply the next worksheet or an endless mantra of 'Good, good, keep going' from a lukewarm adult presence in the classroom, then it is not nearly reward enough to change learning dispositions in the direction of rigour and complexity.

The capacity to differentiate praise is essential for meddling teachers. Praising everything – 'You've brought a biro – oh, well done!' washes out the really tough work of thinking from the menial routine work of following instructions. As elaborated in the next chapter, we have come through an era that has overdone praise in the name of raising self-esteem. Specifically, the desire to make kids 'feel good' has resulted not only in 'results inflation' (everyone has to have an 'A') but also the on-going decline of teachers' professional reputations, while adolescents are rewarded for things that would not tax the smarts of a three-year-old.

As leaders of creative effort in the classroom, meddling teachers are not easily seduced into praising, but when they give it – and they look constantly for opportunities to do so authentically – its effect lasts. When it is given, a student is told what it is for. That student will remember when and why because praise is not easy won and because it is related to a particular thinking achievement.

A teacher who 'meddles-in-the-middle' is active and engaged, and no pushover when it comes to high expectations. Such teachers deeply believe that rigour is sexy, and they have very high expectations that they have a responsibility to induct their students into communities of creative practice, regardless of their ethnic or social background or their past performance on standardised tests. So they set out to catch kids being smart, and keep asking them to be even smarter.

'Do you get wetter standing in the rain or walking in the rain?' This deceptively simply question opens up a raft of experimental possibilities. The Sage-on-the-stage is likely to give the answer and expect students to learn it and regurgitate it at exam time.

The Guide-on-the-Side may become concerned if students begin to show stress when they can't find the solution quickly and receive praise for it. They may respond by giving lots of hints and suggestions. In doing so, they can unwittingly take the challenge out of the task. In doing everything but supply the answer, they can seem supportive, but they steal from their students the opportunity to struggle and make mistakes.

The Meddler-in-the Middle does not rush to save students from the struggle that higher-order thinking involves, by giving them either the answer or the template for finding it. They leave the students in the 'grey' of 'not knowing', supporting any and all attempts on the part of their students to be usefully ignorant. Moreover, they do not presume that the highest achievers in the class are the best learners. Indeed, they anticipate that many of the students who are on the margins of the school culture may have more to offer in terms of creative effort.

They also know that disrupting the passivity that is the enemy of learning is not done best by coaxing or false praise. Nor is it best done by returning to old-fashioned methods of classroom management. It is done best by modelling the pleasure of the rigour of defeating thinking habits. Meddlers-in-the-Middle set up learning environments that optimise the possibilities for doing this, in the full expectation that their students will learn as much from the instructive complications of error-making and uncertainty as they do from finding solutions and getting rewards. Through this sort of pedagogical activity, the students of Meddlers, in John Seely Brown's terms, are 'learning to be' creative workers.[26]

So what?

I am convinced that we need to develop a new teaching identity that resembles a Meddler-in-the-Middle, rather than relying on the techniques of a Sage-on-the-Stage or a Guide-on-the-Side, in order to overcome pedagogical passivity, the enemy of creative capacity building.

Passive non-engagement or a blasé attitude runs counter to the self-managing capacities that John Howkins identified as those of a creative worker (see chapter 2). Self-invention, owning your own ideas, being nomadic, learning endlessly, borrowing, reinventing and recycling – these are all characteristics of a proactive disposition, of self-starters who do not need to be told who they are and what the next move is. A culture of teaching that values obedient attentiveness, or busy work, rather than productive engagement is death to proactive, self-managing learning.

Fortunately, active engagement, rather than listening and regurgitating, reflects the learning preferences of the Yuk/Wow Generation, who prefer trying things out rather than being told what to do. If teachers can understand the value of being 'usefully ignorant' about learning options and possibilities, at the same time as they are expert in their disciplinary field and their pedagogical practice, who are active and inventive in the classroom, who challenge and support, who do not make things too easy, and who are not the only source of authority, who use processes of discovery effectively, who enjoy learning themselves and who do not rush to rescue their students from complexity – such teachers will contribute immeasurably to the creative capacity of their students now and in the future.

In summary, what would we expect of Meddler-in-the-Middle teachers?

↪ That they see themselves as designers of learning opportunities, not just deliverers of 'content' packages. (This does not mean that the curriculum is content-free, but it does mean that the focus is on using content to create new knowledge, not on memorising content.)

↪ That they have clear strategies for helping their students 'know what to do when they don't know what to do'.

↪ That they are good at setting up experiments that might fail (that is, they would welcome error).

↪ That they help kids fail without shame. The victimless classroom is the ideal: everyone in the class is treated with respect, and they learn to give it as well as receive it.

- That they are capable users of digital technology, but they do not rely on it to do the teaching for them. And they are pleased to be taught about the affordances of new technology by the students themselves.
- That they have a good understanding of the culture of all kids. (This means they value cultural diversity in the classroom rather than seeing it as a hurdle to be overcome.)
- That they can bring 'subject', technology and culture together. (For example, an Australian French teacher could use digital technology to link her French class to students in New Caledonia to share cultures as well as opportunities to develop their foreign language skills.)
- That they invite noise, uncertainty and argument as part of the fun of learning.

Many of these characteristics are simply what we would expect from good teachers. However, the stakes are now higher, and this means that hitting just one or two of these buttons is not enough. High-flying young people need teachers who are fast-moving and energetic learners, not just teachers who are pleasant and friendly childminders.

Raising the bar on risk and challenge

What is education for? According to many of today's teachers in training, as well as those currently practising, it is for raising students' self-esteem and helping them reach their full potential. Their 'full potential' may or may not be thought to include creativity, because any evidence of creative capacity is still commonly thought to be some sort of display of artistic talent. This means that many young people might not be deemed to have 'creative' futures, particularly boys who have never warmed to 'girlie stuff' like art or drama.

Whatever 'full potential' means, there is one thing on which many teachers, counsellors and caregivers are likely to agree. The way to raise self-esteem and promote full potential is to ensure that students experience life in positive rather than negative terms. The problem arises when we confuse 'threat' with challenge. If we see every big challenge, every tough choice, every failed project, as a threat to self-esteem, then we conflate threat with challenge. And when we do this we protect students from the confusion and difficulty that is at the heart of real learning.

There is no doubting the importance of positives in lives of young people: positive people around them, positive experiences of social interaction, positive feedback on effort made and goals achieved. Yet accentuating the positive is only part of the story of how self-efficacy – including creative capacity – is built. The part that also needs to be acknowledged is the ability to welcome error and learn from its instructive complications.

Learning is a risky business – it can't be roses all the way. If the creative worker is to have the requisite capacity to be a tough self-regulator, someone who is willing and able to throw passably good work in the bin in order to shoot for more, then affirmation alone won't do it. In fact, piling on the affirmation may be counter-productive, contributing to vulnerability, a preference for 'easy success', and the need for constant reassurance, rather than building emotional and mental robustness.

At a recent Creativity Showcase held for Australian universities,[1] one of the participants, a creative writing expert, reflected wistfully: 'I wish I had an X-ray machine that I could use on every undergraduate who comes in convinced they have a book inside them waiting to pop out. I would X-ray them and say: "No, it's not true – you don't have a book inside you!"' Another spoke of her aim as assisting students to become 'lean, mean, ethical, provoking machines',[2] adaptable to change and confident in questioning conventional thinking and doing.

Other lecturers joined the chorus of concerns about first-year students who expect to have their every effort lauded, whatever the quality, and their opinions validated, whether or not they are informed by scholarly opinion. Teachers in the visual arts lamented the fact that their students had so much to unlearn about sculpture. They expect to be treated as individual geniuses, and they expect their first-time efforts to be given high grades: 'They have difficulty throwing out anything they have done – it's the first time they have not been told their preliminary efforts do not compare favourably with a Rodin.'

For all the good things that psychologist William Glasser's plea advocacy of 'schools without failure' has brought to education,[3] what it has obscured in the process is the importance of error-making in the risky business of learning. While there is merit in the idea that young people will learn better if they are in a supportive environment in which 'significant others' give them reward and recognition, this can be – and has been – a stumbling block when those same young people leave the cloister of the home and the school and move into a less personal and more demanding social world. The teaching examples in the previous chapter show that it is possible to provide direction and support and still open up possibilities for making choices – and making errors.

For many teachers and parents alike, failure and error are now conflated as negatives for their young charges. When opportunities for error-making are eliminated in the service of building self-esteem, then we run the serious risk of protecting young people from learning itself.

Neuroscientists are joining the ranks of those who argue for a more experimental and error-welcoming mode of pedagogical engagement.[4] This marks a shift away from teaching as mere student affirmation. It signals a fundamental shift towards the 'meddling' teaching elaborated in the previous chapter. If students are to be invited to become prod-users of disciplinary and interdisciplinary knowledge, rather than passive recipients of the knowledge of adult others, then they will need to tolerate – indeed welcome – the possibility of making mistakes. They won't avoid them because they only want to hear good things about themselves.

Teaching as therapy

For error-making to become an integral part of our pedagogical processes, there is work to be done to uncouple the snug relationship that currently exists between education and personal therapy. There is a fundamental problem for creative capacity-building when pedagogy is confused with – and then conflated with – therapeutic work. Evidence of this conflation is rampant at all levels of education, from childcare to doctoral studies.

In these more enlightened educational times, informed as they are by humanistic models of social engagement, the student–teacher relationship is less likely than it was half a century ago to be one of oppressor and oppressed. It is much more likely to be shaped by the student expectation that: 'It's my opinion and my offering. Your job as a teacher is to build up my self-esteem. In order to do that, you will give me only positive feedback.' This, to put it somewhat crudely, is the message that teaching-as-therapy has given many of our young people.

The New Zealand-made TV series *Seven Periods with Mr Gormsby* (2006) is a biting satire of contemporary schools for what they are not achieving through therapeutic approaches to the business of educating. For all its outrageous and unapologetic political incorrectness, the Gormsby series targets a genuine problem in the nature and purposes of contemporary schooling. The problem is that, in seeking more student-centredness, more respect for diversity and more community welfare and engagement after the collapse of other social institutions (such as family and church), teaching can come to look more like amateurish therapy than able tuition. It is the latter of these two that is the more likely to improve life outcomes.

When this happens, the educational project is diverted towards ego-protection and away from rigorous thinking and doing. Therapy serves the needs of people who are dysfunctional in certain respects. Most young people do not fit this category: they experience the normal ups and downs of personal growth and of managing social relationships. Only a minority is in need of therapy. Yet we now see the popularity of 'anger management', 'time-outs', learning contracts, counselling and mediation in schools, all testimony to the fact that therapeutic practices are well-established practices in mainstream education.

This means that 'Jason', an imaginary boy who once would have been caned for his expletive response to a teacher's call to attention, is now the subject of much psychological scrutiny about his behaviour: the reasons for it and the means to remediate it. He may be happier to have the cane than to spend so much time wheedling about all this but, in our progressive era, there is a broad consensus that therapy is more moral and ethical strategy for 'managing' Jason than inflicting pain or ignoring the behavioural evidence of his dis/ease altogether.

Some charming absurdities result from this consensus, not the least of which is the astonishingly early age at which young people can take advantage of the vulnerability of adult caregivers and the speed with which teachers have come to imitate psychologists and therapists in their ability to 'see' evidence of vulnerability in the children they teach.

The problem with all this for creative capacity-building is that it sets students up to anticipate and expect a smooth and seamless educational ride when the sort of learning that builds creative capacity is unlikely to be either smooth or seamless. Therapeutic pedagogy can mean, when taken to extremes, that preferred activities and personal comfort come to matter more than enhancing learning. A case in point is the situation observed by a doctoral student conducting research in a primary school where a year 1 student preferred lying on the floor to sitting on a seat. It was noticed by his teacher that his writing (which was relatively advanced on entry) was regressing. This could (and should) have been remediated by the teacher, through telling the boy, 'When we write, we sit on a seat', then requiring him to do so. However, the teacher in this case expressed the view that it was more important for him to stay on the floor 'because he likes it there'. 'The main thing' she said, 'is that he is happy in the classroom.'

Happiness is not unimportant. But 'keeping them happy' is not the same as 'student-centredness'. An effective teacher works in the best interests of their charges, and this may not mean that they are always happy. I have often told my students that my job was to help them be their best selves, and this might mean throwing challenges at them that they would rather avoid. In this case, the little boy in question could easily have been just as happy – and at the same time improving his writing skills – when sitting on a seat. This teacher, with the best of motives, was patronising, not performing the important work of 'expanding [his] capacity to learn'.[5] For Claxton, the antidote to the educational tyrannies of the past lies not in patronising but in 'giving young people whatever-it-is that we think they will need in order to thrive … in the face of the challenges and opportunities … they are going to meet'.[6]

The creative workforce

In taking the personal preferences of young people as the only legitimate criteria for designing learning spaces and developing curriculum, teachers may feel that they are 'supporting' students in every possible way. But they may also be making it easy for themselves and their students to undervalue challenge and to excuse themselves from risk-taking and coping with authentic feedback (including critical feedback) on their best efforts.

So we face a real dilemma in preparing creative workers. We need to ensure that young people get practice in taking risks in order to learn and unlearn, but we also must ensure that we minimise psychological harm, by protecting young people from destabilising or hurtful personal experiences. In the terms of learning scientist John Bruer,[7] president of the James S. McDonnell Foundation, we need to value, create and sustain environments that are low in threat and high in challenge. The examples in chapter 5 could well be seen as exemplars of this type of environment. Learning is tough and learning is fun – it's about a 50/50 split.

A culture of experimentation and error-making does not sit comfortably with an ethos of learning focused narrowly on a personal psychology of remediating vulnerability. The latter is driven by the idea that, the more success experienced, the higher will be the self-esteem, and the student will therefore come to associate learning with personal enjoyment and fulfilment. To endorse confusion, failure and unresolvedness as central elements of the pedagogical process may be seen to be putting the personal well-being of students at risk. Put another way, stretching the intellect and the imagination is risky when protecting students is sacrosanct.

The fact that most schools and universities now offer free therapy sessions to teachers and students to help them cope with the stresses of performing their teaching and learning roles is one effect of the extent to which teaching and learning has become reframed as a form of 'emotional labour'.[8] As counsellor, the teacher loses the authority to punish, but wins the opportunity gently to require a much greater level of personal disclosure from the student. Thus the confessional work of the 'getting to know you' session has become one of the more predictable start-up moments for progressive tutorials. Resistance to such disclosure marks the defensive or inhibited student. Guessing at students' inner life has indeed become an art form in some quarters, with early childhood teachers now on red alert for the tell-tale signs of suicide ideation in children who use black crayons with excessive zeal.

In *Governing the Soul: The Shaping of the Private Self*, cultural theorist Nikolas Rose provides some background to help us understand how pedagogy and therapy have become so inextricably intertwined.[9] He explains how, since World War II, 'psychologically inspired techniques of self-inspection and self-examination' have come to be utilised 'in every area in which human action was to be shaped up', with the result that we now see 'the problems of defining and living a good life ... transposed from an ethical to a psychological register'.[10] This has meant, among other things, a growing fascination on the part of teachers and child caregivers with the inner workings of the self and a growing commitment to a positive personal psychology as the key to educational and social success.

The rise of self-esteem has been very much a symptom of this shift. Steven Ward's *Filling the World with Self-esteem: A Social History of Truth-making* explains how 'self-esteem' has been able to plug into social and political agendas once it had been discovered,[11] well after the term had been invented theoretically by Abraham Maslow in the 1940s. Ward explains that, in the period 1940–70, 'self-esteem became a central concept in experimental and survey studies of ethnocentrism, social class, stress, delinquency, failure motivation and so on'.[12] Once high self-esteem gained the status of 'key to the good life', then raising self-esteem became, at least in theory, the undisputed work of every caring teacher.

The consensus that raising self-esteem is the most important work of teachers ignores evidence that self-esteem can be too high. The idea that most criminals are actually suffering from low self-esteem is a myth. We now know that 'weakness, immaturity and vanity, and an endless capacity for lying' are the hallmarks of criminality,[13] and that low self-esteem is by no means the only culprit when it comes to social pathology.

The problem we face in preparing 21st-century young people for an uncertain and highly complex world is not that young people should undervalue themselves. They will need a robust sense of self-efficacy to work without scripts and to back themselves as capable experimenters. The problem is that a singular focus on self-esteem cannot of itself do all that needs doing with respect to error-making.

When raising self-esteem is overdone, as it often is, young people come to expect instant and on-going success. The first time they experience anxiety or setbacks, they are floored by them. Recent research indicates that academically highly performing students are most likely to be flattened in this way.[14] This is understandable when schools and parents have been fixated on awards, trophies and A pluses, and on keeping children (and especially their daughters) safe at all costs. Winning trophies and playing safe are not the conditions in which creative capacities will thrive.

Teaching as risk minimisation

To make the culture shifts necessary to mitigate the unintended effects of self-esteem and child protection on the future creative workforce, it is important to understand just how hard-wired teachers have become to the roles of risk manager and child protector.

In the 1980s and 1990s, teachers began to experience a much higher level of work regulation through a new generation of programs of professional development and systems of accountability. With the welfare state in full retreat from the funding of education at every level, and the heightened focus on education as both the hope and the despair of parents wanting a guarantee of success for their decreasing numbers of children, the teacher became the target of newly explicit performance criteria as a professional classroom manager providing high-quality client services in 'more-for-less' times.

Management in 'more-for-less' times is not about taking risks but avoiding them. According to sociologist Anthony Giddens, the late twentieth and early twenty-first centuries have been characterised by a political and moral climate of danger minimisation.[15] 'Risk society', the term Ulrich Beck uses to describe this climate,[16] is all about paying attention to the negatives; it is a shift away from the management and distribution of material or industrial 'goods' to the management and distribution of economic and social 'bads'. The focus is on what can go wrong, rather than on learning from the instructive complications of error-making.

In performing the role of risk managers, teachers have come to use a new generation of systemic tools, rules, formats and technology for communicating with educational authorities, employers, parents and each other. Armed with such paraphernalia, 'expert' teachers seek to solve any and every potential 'trouble', real or imagined.

An effect of all this has been a heightened pressure on teachers to be data vacuum cleaners in schools, never missing an opportunity to make additions to profile data that defines the student as a case of (more or less) potential risk. Statistical correlations of heterogeneous elements differentiate student 'risk' categories – low SES, LOTE, indigenous, learning disabled, rural and remote, and so on – each demanding appropriate interventions according to the risks associated with that population category.

This makes for a much more complex educational environment than existed when teachers were relatively autonomous inside the walls of the classroom and students were fixed in one place. The contemporary school has children moving in and out of classrooms to spend time with specialists who can treat their dysfunction or remediate their learning disability on a one-to-one or small group basis. This specialist treatment is laudable for a host of reasons, not the least of which is that more children are now considered educable than was once the case. However, the forensic work of identifying vulnerabilities and minimising risks has militated against risk-taking as an important element of the pedagogical work in classrooms.

Where to from here?

Young people ought to feel protected, and they ought to feel a sense of self-efficacy. However, a home or school environment characterised by unrelenting affirmation and risk minimisation is not one that is adequate to their learning needs as future creatives. Whatever is done, it needs to be done carefully in the full knowledge of how much has already been invested in building up self-esteem and removing risk, and the damage that could be done by pulling these platforms away. So what might be done?

A useful starting point for considering how to move beyond merely affirming and protecting young people is provided by social psychological researcher and educator Carol Dweck. Dweck makes a clear distinction between what she terms 'learning goals' and 'performance goals'. As she puts it, an individual's performance goals are focused on 'winning positive judgment of your competence and avoiding negative ones', while an individual's learning goals are characterised by a desire to develop 'new skills, master new tasks or understand new things'.[17]

While both sorts of goals are 'normal and universal', they can be – and often are – in conflict. Dweck explains that, when there is an overemphasis on performance goals – as is increasingly the case for the present generation of young people – individuals are less likely to extend their zones of competence, and more likely to blame their own lack of ability if things go wrong. In worrying about their own lack of ability, they fail to give attention to strategy. When the pressure is on, if they can't look smart, nothing matters more than avoiding looking dumb, and this can consume a great deal of time and energy, while at the same time creating a downward spiral of self-recrimination, vulnerability and victimhood.[18]

In Dweck's research on the performance and learning activities of young people, performance goals and learning goals were found to be present in most of these individuals in about a 50/50 ratio. They can, however, be manipulated by an influential external 'other' (such as a parent, trainer or teacher). When this occurs, the students for whom learning goals are paramount continue to seek new strategies and to tolerate error without self-blame, while those who are performance-driven are more likely to give up on the task set, berating themselves for their inability to complete it.

In practice, this means that a child who was being encouraged to learn juggling might, if healthily learning-oriented, approach the task by considering a number of strategies. They might appropriately decide that listening to a lecture on juggling might not be as useful as trial and error attempts with just two balls. Once they feel competent with two, they may move to three. When they drop the balls, as they will frequently do, they know that the problem is that they have not yet had enough practice and that they will need regular and longer rehearsals to acquire juggling skill. They do not think they are stupid for being unable to juggle. It is finding a successful strategy that matters.

This approach to capacity-building stands in sharp contrast with that of the child who is too highly performance-oriented. Their approach is more likely to be characterised by fear of trying something in which they might fail, giving up when it seems that the skill of juggling cannot be quickly and easily acquired, and blaming themselves for being so 'bad' at it. Long-term, this disposition to refuse a learning challenge can means an increasingly truncated set of skills in the young person who comes to resist new learning, greater anxiety when presented with new challenges and greater inflexibility about what they perceive they can or cannot do: 'I'm only good at maths or rugby – if it's anything else, forget it!'

By implication, teachers or parents who stress performance above all else – by means of trophies, awards or test results – encourage their students to be overly focused on winning positive judgment from external others, and this puts them at risk in relation to their openness to learning new skills and strategies. Conversely, teachers and parents who seek to foster a healthy balance of learning goals and performance goals encourage robust learners who can stick at a task. They do not need easy or instant success and constant reassurance in order to have a sense of self-efficacy.

If, as Dweck points out, the tasks that are best for learning are those that risk confusion and error, then pedagogical work directed at improved learning outcomes will concentrate on the instructive complications that arise from making mistakes. Error is welcomed and up-front explanation minimised. Everyone is interested in staying with and learning from the problem, not finding the quick solution. Where error results in painful condemnation from external others who are marking, grading and measuring each move, then it is more likely that a student will stay within a very narrow field of activity and shoot for easy success within that field, avoiding any situation that takes them away from their zone of expertise and emotional comfort.

Teaching for creativity will also involve helping young people to be explicit about, as well as responsible for, their learning goals by differentiating them from their performance goals. A learning goal is not 'to get a higher grade in English' or to come top in maths, but to be able to construct a strong argument using evidence and to understand and be able to apply the basic principles of statistical calculation. It should also involve learning not just things that are not closely associated with traditional educational knowledge but also a wide and diverse set of learning challenges from rock-climbing to rap-dancing. When students know that their teacher values the totality of their learning, not just their test results, then students are more likely to value learning, not just performing.

Taking responsibility for learning goals does not happen at parent–teacher meetings where the actual learner and performer is absent and being talked about. It is more likely to result from both teacher and parent listening with respect and attention to a student's account of what they have or have not achieved and why, in relation to the strategies they have used or are developing. When young people know that they are being asked to take responsibility for the learning and to provide evidence in support of their claims, they are much more likely to enhance the scope of their learning and the quality of their performance.

A working disposition

How does this translate in the workplace? Frank Madero, in his book *How to Get the Job You Want* describes the attitudes that make the difference to being employed or not.[19] His descriptions are closely aligned with the differences Dweck identifies between those overly focused on themselves and what they can or can't perform (a negative) and those who have a healthy learning goal disposition (a positive):

> In many workplaces there are workers who can ride the good and the bad, but also those who will spend a lot of energy on the negatives. These types don't progress too far with their jobs. A worker with a positive attitude would say: 'I know what we have to achieve and although I haven't got the answer just yet, we'll achieve it somehow.' A worker with a lousy attitude might respond to the same situation with: 'That's too hard, it's impossible and I don't want to try.'[20]

Young people who are overly focused on performance may well project a combination of arrogance and vulnerability that is certainly off-putting in a workplace situation. In needing to be right all the time, they can be dismissive of colleagues who are prepared to try a new way of doing things: 'A positive attitude ... means not having to be right all the time. Anyone who continually needs to be right runs the serious risk of damaging their relationships, both professional and personal. [Good employees are] accepting of others' beliefs even when they are completely at odds with your own.'[21]

Helping young people to focus on strategy rather than on themselves is a way to ensure that young people are emotionally resilient, positive and employable. If the tendency is for children to hunker down and shoot for easy success, the effective teacher, parent or caregiver will help them stay with a task, supporting and praising their stickability and their preparedness to be tough self-critics rather than praising their 'products'.

So what might this look like in practice? I was fortunate enough to come across an example recently when working with teachers in a professional learning program (see example 6.1).

It is not easy for young people who are used to being the focus of adoring adult attention to unlearn 'easy success'. Successful creative effort demands constant pruning, just as a garden is enhanced by the constant removal of plant material, not just by sowing seeds and standing back. The ability to discern and then reject a merely passable effort, to be self-critical, to strive for something even better – these are not capacities that are easily developed or easily 'sold'. They actually

Example 6.1 Building stickability

Teachers in a secondary school art department offered to teach art to the 10-year-olds in the primary school across the road. 'We'll get them to do a painting – it'll take about six weeks,' they told the year 5 teachers. The year 5 teachers made it clear at the outset that they believed the children would not be prepared to spend that long doing one painting. 'They'll have it done fast', they said, 'and they will expect it to be put up on the wall just as fast!'

True enough, most of the 10-year-olds were 'finished' within the first half-hour and wanted instant recognition and reward for their paintings. The secondary art teachers did not tell them their paintings were wonderful. They did not put the paintings on display or hand out prizes. Instead, they held the young artists in the activity by commenting on the 'work-in-progress'. 'Let's look at what you've done very closely. Your tree branches are straight lines. Now let's go out and look at a real tree – see how the branches narrow as they move away from the trunk. Let's try that again and see if it can be more like a real tree branch.' Finally, after helping the 10-year-olds to 'stay in the grey' and accept that more work can and should be done, teachers did enable most of them to produce artistic work of a high standard. Moreover, and perhaps more importantly, they provided the 10-year-olds with a much more authentic entrée into the work of an artist than they were getting in a world where their every effort was met with undifferentiated praise.

The children began to understand, in Seely Brown's terms,[22] what it meant to 'be artistic', including how much 'product' needs to be jettisoned and how important it is to be able to make their own judgments about it, regardless of their opinion of their own 'talent' or the time they had taken.

require courage from within as well as the courage to give support and direction from without.

Courage, as cognition expert Guy Claxton reminds us, is a much-overlooked aspect of 'creativity-as-wisdom':

> To act wisely might well take a degree of courage: daring to intervene in situations that are emotionally fraught or downright dangerous, rather than hanging back or merely theorising or pontificating from a position of personal safety; and to do so in ways that others might find strange.

This might in turn require a degree of indifference to public opinion – reflecting a secure sense of self, perhaps – and a commitment to doing what 'feels right' rather than what 'looks good'.[23]

It does take courage for a young person to persist when all the messages they have had in their short lives tell them that success is easy and that reward is and ought to be close at hand. It also takes courage for teachers, parents and caregivers to withstand the criticisms, tears or tantrums that may follow when a child is frustrated by 'not knowing' and not being rescued or affirmed early and often.

This is not meant as an endorsement of the much-vaunted 'no pain, no gain' formula that is wrongly used to justify throwing a youngster into the deep end of the pool or otherwise frightening them into competence. If therapeutic approaches are being overused, inappropriate or counter-productive, they are certainly preferable to learning through trauma.

The sort of courage Claxton speaks of is not to be confused with foolhardiness. Claxton himself warns about the growing incidence of 'teenage recklessness and escapism, the rising statistics of adolescent depression and anxiety and of self-harm and suicidal thoughts'.[24] He goes on to say that 'mopping up distress with chemicals or counselling doesn't get to the heart of the matter', which, for him, is the challenge of ensuring that young people have the resources that an expanded capacity to learn gives them for dealing with the confusion and uncertainty of 21st-century living.

Counsellors in schools have an unenviable job in supporting the many young people who have been victims of trauma, who come from chaotic or abusive households or who do not learn in the same way as most of us. However, as many school counsellors now attest, among the school dropouts, school resisters or learning disabled students they support, there is now a burgeoning group of children who have just received their first 'B' on an assignment or a test.

The anxiety of the child in the face of this setback is often eclipsed by the 'devastation' felt by their parents. 'How can this be? She/he has never got less than an A.' There must be some mistake – either that or the child is not really as 'bright' as was shown by the 'gifted and talented' test. Academic hopes and aspirations are in tatters. Because parents are increasingly taking on the role of their children's 'learning managers' – searching the internet for information, locating the best software, paying for the best coaching, and diligently following the criteria of every test instrument – the stakes and the familial anxiety are very high indeed.

Supportive and empathic parents have always been an asset to young learners. However, when parents had families of five or more children, and when schools and universities were relatively 'closed' or alienating places, fewer adults had the time or inclination to be 'helicopter parents', hovering over their children in any and every performative moment. In the one-child families that are now the norm in the West rather than the exception, an individual child carries the entire weight of expectation of the upward social mobility of the family – or at least the expectation of maintaining or enhancing the level of security and status already achieved. When feted as a little emperor in their own home, the only child has a mountain to climb in the less cosseted social world in which they will need to function when they walk out the door. They will have to cope with the negative judgments of others – or, perhaps more difficult still, the indifference of others – and still maintain a sense of positive self-worth.

Teachers and lecturers know what this means as evaluators of student performance, and can attest to academic inflation as a fact of educational life. On a seven-point scale, a 'satisfactory' assignment is now perceived by many students to be worth a credit, not a pass, so assessors are being placed increasingly under pressure to concede a higher grade. This means more disputation, more complaints, more time taken in justifying a grade or in re-marking. 'If only they would put as much work into the assignment as they do into their case for a review of their grade', lecturers lament, 'we would not be going through any of this!' It is not that complaining about low grades is anything new. What is new is that it has become so commonplace and so potentially litigious.

It is a courageous teacher who encourages risk-taking in such litigious and compliance-driven times. The incitements to risk-taking and daring that are now so well embedded in the creativity literature can underplay how much cultural resistance to risk-taking abounds in formal education.[25] Celebrating its importance is one thing, but enacting it in the context of a litigious society and a timid teaching profession, and heightened concerns about the vulnerability of young people from all sectors of society, is quite another.

Sociologist Chris Jenks attributes much of the heightened anxiety around the 'postmodern child' to fears that spring from adult nostalgia for lost certainties: 'our collective pain at our loss of social identity'.[26] The argument he makes is that we fill the lives of young people with anxieties about their vulnerability because we hanker for the social stability of a community that no longer exists – at least not in the form that many of us once experienced.

Where once it was accepted that caring parents might let their children roam a neighbourhood as long as they were back before dark, now the idea that unaccompanied children might be out riding their pushbike, or digging in the local creek or playing in a local park, is enough to generate high levels of anxiety in many parents. It is no accident that our houses are expanding to include a larger number of places where children can be under constant surveillance. The fact that our children have never been safer from stranger danger, statistically speaking, is no consolation. Media catastrophising and an endless array of parental self-help books and services keep parents convinced of the growing threat of harm in what is portrayed as an increasingly hostile and uncaring world.

Whether or not we agree with Jenks's theory that 'child panic'[27] has more to do with adult anxiety than real child vulnerability, it is difficult to argue with the proposition that risk-taking demands courage: the courage to cross incommensurate and unknown activity domains, to work with incompatibles, to keep alternative pathways open, to cope with rejection. Courage is not something we expect from young people by and large. We are surprised when we see them being courageous, and we may feel uneasy when it occurs, fearing that the child's exposure may be harmful rather than helpful.

If courage is a quality that is worth fostering in the service of creative capacity-building, so too is self-assertiveness. Our tendency to conflate assertiveness with aggression, and that in turn with malevolence, can obscure the importance of what ethicist Brian Masters calls 'benign personal aggressiveness'.[28] Masters argues that the rapacious appetite for new experiences that characterises creative entrepreneurs like Richard Branson is mobilised by a form of aggressiveness that is not stifled by ordinariness or diminished by the passing of time.

From a very early age, Branson's relentless pursuit of new challenges saw him setting up a vast business empire at the same time that he achieved world record feats in travel of various kinds. Speaking of Branson's whirlwind personal journey, Masters says: 'Richard Branson perfectly illustrates the positive power of benign personal aggressiveness … [He] has been lucky to the extent that nothing has tended to check his natural assertiveness. Had he been stumped by bad heredity, hostile social circumstances, cruel upbringing or a temperament prone to morosity and mental hesitancy, he would have turned out quite differently.'[29]

There is nothing teachers can do about the heredity of their students. There is little they can do about the social circumstances into which they were born. But there is much they can do to contribute to their disposition to learn. Teachers embody for their students what a learner looks like. If teachers are 'mentally hesitant' in the face of change, or if they seem paralysed by what they do not control or cannot do, then they are teaching young people lessons that are unhelpful when it comes to creative futures.

If teachers seem like 'losers', then we cannot expect young people to value the nature of their business – the business of learning. If, on the other hand, teachers challenge the maxim of G. B. Shaw that 'those who can do, and those who can't teach', by exhibiting a zest for life and a productive personal power that translates into active engagement, risk-taking and experimentation, they give their students a much greater chance of learning to be a creative 'doer'. This is more than just being 'positive' or displaying a falsely cheerful demeanour. Students can see through this sort of performance very easily indeed. It may mean allowing students to see the disappointment and confusion that teachers also feel at times when experiments fail. But it should not mean a retreat from risk.

The sort of pedagogy that fosters 'creative doing' is provided by Julie White, a teacher educator at the University of Melbourne (see example 6.2).[30]

Example 6.2 Encouraging risk-taking

As she elaborates it,[31] White and her colleagues made an explicit commitment to risk-taking in training primary and secondary teachers. 'The focus of the program was on allowing teachers to explore their own creativity by daring to dance and sing – even though they didn't have particular talent in these areas.'

The lecturers' rationale for their pedagogical design was that, as future teachers, their students would need to nurture creativity in their own students, so they needed 'some experience of creativity themselves'.

The students worked in groups to create 'arias of learning'. The arias of learning were operatic episodes designed as 'complex combinations of the theoretical, the practical, the personal and the political' through which students could come to terms with such dichotomies as 'the emotional and intellectual, power and powerlessness, knowledge and ignorance'.

The result was a number of 'ethnographic, operatic performances' by the students that elaborated key issues 'focused on learning about pedagogy and curriculum'.

For the students, this was a risky business indeed: 'I had never done any sort of public performance. Singing, acting and dancing certainly did not sit happily in my comfort zone.'

Despite initial reluctance borne of fear and or lack of experience, most students did come to appreciate the fact that what they were being asked to do was highly relevant to the pedagogical work they would soon be doing as professionals. '[W]e were a mixed group consisting mainly of virgin performers who had not been involved in a lot of performing arts before ... We all seemed to feel that the process was one of learning fast on your feet (a lot like teaching, really).'

The 'outcomes' were not universally positive for all. This is also part of the risk that a teacher takes when embarking on innovative pedagogical work. Yet even those whom White identifies as finding the process 'unsatisfactory' do not seem untouched by its significance to their learning: 'The opera was not "framed" enough for me as a learner ... I think I am still confused, but the process will stick with me throughout my teaching career as an annoyingly unfinished jigsaw puzzle connecting staff, students and external influences of education.'

For all the positive feedback about the value of letting go, and the excitement of taking the risk, perhaps the strongest testament to the value of this exercise is the confusion and annoyance that lingered for the student deemed by the researchers to have found the experience 'unsatisfactory'. Many students remembered the pleasure of the engagement and minimising or downplaying the discomfort they felt in taking on such an 'unnatural' activity as performing an opera. Where the memory of experiencing and learning to live with discomfort lingers as 'an annoyingly unfinished jigsaw puzzle', there may well be a more sustained change in the thinking and doing of the trainee teacher who provided this feedback. The recognition of this learning as 'unfinished business' is a healthy sign of an expanded disposition to consider learning as on-going. Finally, it is not about achieving mastery but of refusing any predefined level of mastery as the end of learning.

So what more might we make of student feedback? This is a sticking point for teachers at a time when positive student feedback is one of their approved performance indicators. Teachers who are confronting, interventionist and idiosyncratic, who ask for more than students expect to give, may find themselves rated lower than those who make more predictable demands of their students. People can and do avoid classes where the teacher has a reputation for being tough when it comes to grades, even if it means they will miss out on the best teaching. Passivity and compliance mean comfort, and comfort means an easier institutional life for all.

Moving away from comfort

Moving out of one's comfort zone often involves physical movement out of familiar locations, as well as a capacity to work within diverse cultural contexts. And this, in turn, draws on the capacity to leave the familiar behind and embrace the unfamiliar. The urge to be 'on the move', to refuse the comforts of home for the discomfort but potential opportunity of distant and exotic places and people, has characterised many of our pioneers and activists. This nomadic impulse is argued to be a more harmonious way to live in the natural environment than the sedentary life most of us have come to live in modern times.[32] Whether or not we agree that nomadism makes for more human virtue, in general terms, than does settlement, the fact remains that creative minds are less likely to tolerate a predictable yet mediocre existence and more likely to take their chances in another location living a different kind of working life.

With the demand for high-level candidates in the business world outstripping supply,[33] and with management positions increasingly requiring a peripatetic lifestyle from those who once merely reached the big office and stayed there, the preparedness to move away from comfort, to risk temporary dislocation in search of greater job satisfaction and better quality of life, may appear to an older generation to look like impatience and, to borrow from *Macbeth*, 'vaulting ambition which o'er leaps itself'. However, the restless energy that so often accompanies the creative worker is also the positive energy that has them settling for no less than the biggest challenge and the most innovative solutions.

Gonzalo Arellano, a game developer and animator in Melbourne, describes his own career pathway in precisely these terms: 'Neither [arts nor computing courses] really clicked with me. I wandered a bit without a real career path, working in a range of unrelated jobs that weren't satisfying, from being a croupier at Crown Casino to working in insurance companies. [I was] still searching for something I was passionate about …'[34]

In 2003 Arellano returned to university, where he began a masters degree in multimedia that included 3D graphics and animation. Although he had been an avid gamer as an adolescent, the world of the games industry was now unfamiliar to him: 'When I started … I had no idea what was going on in the games industry – I barely knew what an Xbox was – so I did plenty of research and have now developed a healthy passion for games … When I started my internship, 90% of my work was animation. Now I have branched out into other areas such as rendering, which brings together all the animation layers and other aspects.'[35]

It might be tempting to extrapolate from the life experiences of 'creatives' like Branson or Arellano that the function of formal education is either not to 'get in the way' of a natural propensity to creative effort or to provide a smorgasbord of possible elective options that can be tapped into whenever and wherever the candidate chooses. To come to this conclusion is to underestimate what formal education might contribute to preparing people for creative futures. The next chapter makes explicit how formal learning environments might become more relevant to a new generation of potential 'creatives'.

So what?

Learning is risky, not just rosy. And this is something that the Yuk/Wow Generation struggles with, because they have been brought up on a diet of praise, or at least the absence of criticism. So they are not always good at taking risks, and are likely to lack the capacity to be tough self-critics. The current 'therapeutic' ethos that pervades many schools is contributing to this problem, in that it is tending to confuse caring with overprotection. This confusion is also reflected in many home environments, where anxious Gen X parents with good intentions want so much for their little ones that they may do far too much for them. The policy climate of risk minimisation exacerbates the problem.

To overcome the problem of 'too much praise, too little challenge', we need to ensure that young people focus on their learning goals (strategies for acquiring new skills and knowledge), not just their performance goals (how they meet the demands of external others). If they can do this, they will make better employees because they put self-management of their learning first and their ego second. The job of teachers, trainers and employers is to build 'stickability' in young people so that they can be more courageous about welcoming the discomfort that comes from uncertainty and ambiguity. Together we can help them build a proactive disposition to learning and critique so that, instead being paralysed when they first taste adversity, they can be astute judges of the value of that feedback for their learning and earning.

Flying higher

In December 2007, the world mourned the passing of Austrian-born Italian designer Ettore Sottsass, famous for his capacity to take commonplace things and imbue them with new meaning. Sottsass successfully pursued two parallel projects: that of giving 'dignity to the mundane' while at the same time creating objects with 'the emotional intensity of art'.[1] A highly gifted architect, he was relentlessly on the move, knowing everyone and working everywhere. His studios produced everything from television sets to precious glassware, from fashion shops for Esprit to calculators for Olivetti, and from household furniture to a golf resort for the People's Liberation Army in China.

Journalist David Sudjic describes his legacy in the following way:

> Sottsass showed that it was possible to understand design as a cultural as well as a technical issue. When he designed the Valentine portable typewriter for Olivetti in 1969 … he was able to turn a piece of office equipment into a desirable object by understanding that there are emotions involved in the way that we use and understand our

The creative workforce

possessions. Sottsass made the Valentine out of bright red plastic, with twin splashes of vivid orange for the spools, turning it from a machine into a kind of toy.[2]

Sottsass was a high-flyer in every sense of the word. He was not limited by cultural conventions, location or language, but was able to transcend the boundaries of thinking and doing that rein in the imagination. He was a border crosser, culturally agile, hungry for challenge and untameable in his quest to combine aesthetics and functionality.

A less well-known 'high-flyer', Ben, is a young man who worked for several years in a growing Queensland audio-technology company, Acoustic Technologies Electronics. The company had an opportunity to generate a long-term business partnership with the Queensland Conservatorium of Music, beginning with the provision of a new sound system in its concert hall. The director of music technology wanted a sound system that was conceptually innovative: aesthetically unique, and delivering the highest quality sound. This was a very important commission for Acoustic Technologies Electronics. The CEO called on Ben, a graduate of the conservatorium, to be a key member of the creative team responsible for designing and installing the unique sound system, not because Ben was the most senior or most experienced member of his production team but because he was passionate and excited about the challenge, and had a record of taking on difficult, new projects and delivering high-level problem-solving. He was also passionate about the project because he had maintained strong relationships with the conservatorium staff, so he was able to straddle the needs of the two organisations involved. The Queensland Conservatorium now has a great asset in its attractive and functional speaker system and Acoustic Technologies Electronics has enhanced its competitive edge, not just in Australia but also worldwide. The speaker boxes Ben designed, although large enough to deliver the power needed to fill a concert hall, appear to float in mid-air above the audience, delicately arched and pleasing to look at as well as to listen to.

Two things were necessary for this successful outcome. They were Ben's capacity to respond to the challenge of imagining a good design, and the team environment in which Ben was part of the production of something unique, requiring innovative thinking and doing, not imitative thinking and doing.

A 'creative' curriculum

In Daniel Pink's terms, the products that both Ben and Sottsass have designed are tangible evidence of the 'high-concept/high-touch' skills that are required in our present 'Conceptual Age'.[3] Unlike the Information Age, whose core business has been the routine accessing of information to solve routine problems, the Conceptual Age invests in, and springs from, new cultural forms and modes of consumption. Sottsass's prolific design output and Ben's contribution to a creative audio-production team both serve as global and local examples of unique form and meaning; that is, beautiful and practical products that combine the creative skill of the artisan and the empathic creativity of the designer.

In his book *A Whole New Mind* Pink makes explicit the 'high-concept' and 'high-touch' capacities that such 'high-flyers' as Sottsass possess to an exceptional degree. 'High-concept' capacities include the ability to create artistic and emotional beauty, to detect patterns and opportunities, to craft a satisfying narrative, and to combine seemingly unrelated ideas into a novel invention. 'High-touch' capacities include the ability to empathise, to understand the subtleties of human interaction, to find joy in oneself and elicit it in others, and to stretch beyond the normal in pursuit of purpose and meaning.

Pink goes further than simply describing the nature of the abilities he identifies as the key capacities needed for living and working in the Conceptual Age. He sets out a 'curriculum' for developing such capacities, a distilled version of which is represented in figure 7.1.

A plethora of implications arise from Pink's framework for building a curriculum for creative capacity-building. First, the skills and capacities named inside the square are those that we generally learn as part of a traditional education. We learn functional literacy and numeracy in English and mathematics. We learn to use evidence to make an argument that has scientific plausibility. We learn to focus

The creative workforce

Figure 7.1
High-concept/high-touch skills (adapted from Pink 2005)

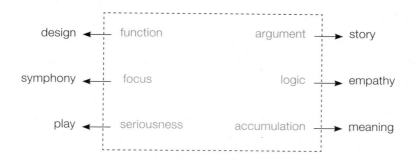

on a topic area through paying attention to the nature and purpose of disciplinary boundaries. We learn logical coherent development of an idea or experiment. We learn that engaging in the processes of learning and schooling is a serious business (as elaborated in chapter 3). And we learn that the intelligent accumulation of facts is important to other forms of accumulation, including cultural, economic and social capital. These domains of knowledge continue to be important to living and working in the Conceptual Age. However, they are by no means sufficient to a creative capacity-building curriculum.

Creative capacity-building requires those elements outside the square – design, story, empathy, play, symphony and meaning – to be understood not as garnish to the content roast but as part of the new roast through which creative capacity is nourished. It also requires a much closer engagement with issues of intellectual property than traditional school curricula have bothered with in the past, because the sort of creative labour that Pink is pre-empting needs an appropriate financial and regulatory architecture. Few adults, let alone young people, have a grasp of this complex issue; nor do they understand the range of licences that are available for copyrighting creative products and under what conditions they might be best utilised.[4]

Let us look more closely at each of Pink's elements of the creativity 'curriculum' in turn.

Design includes – but is not synonymous with – function in that it gives shape and meaning to our lives in ways unprecedented in nature, combining utility and significance in our living and working environments. Unfortunately, education is one domain of social life that has been starved of the benefits of living with and drawing on good design, given that 'beauty has long taken a backseat to bureaucracy'[5] in government-funded enterprises. The lack of good design in our publicly funded schools and colleges – peeling paint, wall-charts stuck up amateurishly with Blu Tack, the functional minimalism of the desks, chairs, classrooms, assembly areas and grounds, the lack of greenery and the lack of evidence of proud user ownership – all this militates against much of the pleasure of learning for the Yuk/Wow Generation, who are much more used to having good design integrated into their everyday lives. When education environments are a 'yuk' experience, it makes it harder for young people to believe that learning can and ought to be a 'wow' experience.

Story is an important corollary to argument and to function. As Pink notes, fact-finding is now so easy that 'an English-speaking 13-year-old in Zaire with an internet connection can find out the current temperature in Brussels, or closing price of IBM stock or name of Winston Churchill's second finance minister as quickly as the head librarian in Cambridge University'.[6] What *story* adds is an emotional component that enriches information. Indigenous cultures have understood this much better than a hyper-rational Western culture that has looked to 'the facts' to understand the world. The Victorians sought to understand 'butterflyness' by filling museum drawers with every sort of dead butterfly they could find, pinned from smallest to largest. This is one way to understand 'butterflyness'. However, it does not tell the story of how butterflyness is experienced when we watch living butterflies fluttering in a garden or a rainforest. We feel something; we don't just observe them or count them.

So too we are coming to understand that health and well-being are not just about identifying the anatomical source of the pain and attempting to eliminate it but also implicate the story of a life being lived. Pink calls this capacity to draw on broad life histories in the

The creative workforce

interests of improving a particular aspect of living 'narrative competence'; that is, 'the ability to absorb, interpret and respond to stories'.[7] While formal education provides opportunities for such story-telling, they are limited in what counts as a story suitable for 'show and tell'. Essay-writing in particular has delimited what counts as a 'good story' by imposing a linear–cumulative model of rationality on story-telling: introduction, paragraphs (point, evidence, relevance) and conclusion. When a potentially creative moment of story-telling is recuperated in a formulaic and routine exercise that meets certain preordained criteria (such as being logical, coherent and technically correct), then much of the juice of living is lost.

As Ken Robinson has pointed out, this straitjacketing of creativity increases exponentially as we move from the crèche to the university.[8] It is not that technical imprecision should be encouraged. Rather, the problem is that what counts as imprecision is so narrowly defined. Put another way, Lewis Carol's 'Jabberwocky' would be unlikely to pass the 'good writing' test today. In David Mulcahy's terms, we are not achieving a higher standard of narrative but a higher standard of standardness![9]

Symphony, as Pink explains it, takes us beyond a singular focus such as we might have in a particular discipline or specialism to see potential relationships between things and people that may be obscure or rendered invisible by our ways of seeing and compartmentalising the world. In seeing possibilities for integrating entities differently, we are better equipped to cross boundaries, milk metaphors, blend concepts and invent 'third space' possibilities of the sort that were mentioned earlier in the discussion of small 'C' creativity in chapter 2.

Just as *design* transcends function, so *empathy* transcends logic. *Empathy* redresses what Pink calls the 'autistic' elements of a computerised and hyper-rational world that is distrustful of intuition or feeling. In this sense it augments factual or procedural professional intelligence, knowledge and competence with a propensity to see the world as others see it. Professional excellence is now argued to be characterised by warmth, rather than distance, power-sharing rather than domination, and coaching rather than coercion and control.[10] This new model of leaderly performance augments rather than detracts from organisational efficiency and good managerial practice, by bringing to it the capacity to listen and pay attention to more than one's own self-interest.

Empathy may thus be viewed as a form of emotional intelligence. However, we should be cautious about swallowing wholesale scripts for developing emotional intelligence that frame the emotions as calculable (in the form of emotional intelligence quotient or EQ). When intelligence quotient (IQ) was held to be the key to social and economic success, it was very quickly held to be calculable, so much was made of IQ test results and what they connoted in terms of a successful future. Now that we have begun to understand the limitations of the rationality of the intellect, and the importance of emotionality in decision-making, leadership and learning, EQ 'measurement' is coming into vogue.[11] In insisting that empathy is calculable as EQ, we are reapplying the very logic that reduced our understanding of intelligence to IQ. While we should laud attempts to make *empathy*, like creativity, less mysterious, we need to ensure that we do not extract the nerve from *empathy* by reducing it to a quick and dirty skill that can be trained in the same way that one can be trained to use a piece of software. *Empathy* is a moral and ethical capacity as well as a capability that can be best observed in and through relational action.

Play, as explained in chapter 3, is a much misunderstood and trivialised human action. Pink endorses Pat Kane's view of *play* as the sort of progressive, imaginative, self-interested, ritualistic, frivolous, carnivalesque and cosmic activity that allows us to be 'energetic, imaginative and confident in the face of an unpredictable, contestive, emergent world'.[12] As Kane sees it, education has been unable to understand or endorse the value of the 'play ethic' because it has 'slipped between a Romantic and a utilitarian model' of play, dividing off '"rational and irrational" recreations'.[13] In doing so it has disallowed – and disavowed – the value of play as a 'multi-literacy' that is invaluable for 21st-century life and work. Kane says:

> We need a new way to look at the complexity of the educational
> experience – one that regards the apparent 'messiness' and 'imprecision'

of play as a deep resource for understanding, rather than something which has to be squeezed out of curricula tailored to deliver better performance statistics for short-termist politicians. I suggest that scholars might unite around a new notion of literacy – a 'multi-literacy' that ties together the deep humanism of the teaching profession with the ludic realities that face their students in the new century.[14]

Kane goes on the make the important point that the 'play ethic' does not serve solely the economic interests of business organisations but a proliferation of interests and networks – 'emotional and sexual, geographical and traditional, artistic and civic'[15] – that are relevant to the fully functioning 21st-century citizen. 'Having fun' has always been somewhat subversive, because fun is not so easily harnessed by those who would either exploit it or bring it to a halt. As apparently inconsequential activity, *play* may or may not turn into something useful, so it is at the same time both potentially dissolute (we end up with nothing to show and time wasted) and/or potentially practical (a winning combination of business and pleasure).

A good example of how this could be done is provided by a teacher who decided that the fun that his boys were having throwing paper planes rather than attending to their science lesson could become something useful in the way of learning about aerodynamics. So he challenged them to set and achieve a goal with their paper planes. Did they want their plane to fly higher, or further, or loop-the-loop and so on? He set up trials, with a final competition at the end of the week to see who had done best to achieve their chosen goal. The boys did not stop having fun, but the play became more purposive and the learning – when and how they needed it – did not seem like a chore. It was instead a means for them to play – and perform – better. Not all of them went on to engage more closely with physics in the following year, but a number did show interest for the first time in one aspect of a subject that, until then, had eluded them.

Meaning, Pink's last contribution to a creativity-building curriculum for the Conceptual Age, comes as an acknowledgment that accumulation of money and goods is not enough to sustain a human being. Whether as spirituality or as happiness, he argues, the search for meaning is fundamental to a life well lived. Pink makes the point that rising abundance and prosperity are allowing more people than those in religious orders to pursue meditation and other techniques for 'going beyond the self'.[16]

What all of Daniel Pink's 'high-touch' elements of curriculum share, as elaborated above, is that they are the most likely to be lopped off when the credentialling heat is turned up, downgraded to the status of 'frills' or 'extras' to be picked up during leisure hours as hobbies. Just as six-year-olds have learned, by the time that they are 10, that you do not stop in a foot-race if the friend who is running with you falls over, so too most young people have learned by age 10 that the high-stakes knowledge domains are English, maths and science and that everything else pales into insignificance next to the Big Three. Story-telling, making models and having fun become distant memories from the early years of education, not to be confused with the 'important' tasks of performing on standard tests.

This is the logic that Daniel Pink rightly seeks to overturn. He insists that the traditional or 'core' knowledge domains are no more or less valuable than the non-traditional knowledge outside the square. (The term 'non-traditional' is not actually helpful here, given the importance of design, story, empathy, play, symphony and meaning-making to indigenous cultures with a much longer shelf-life than cosmopolitan cultures.) Most importantly, Pink argues the value of holding both sorts of knowledge together in the interests of building the sort of capacity that Sottsass so brilliantly exemplified. The ability to think and do in ways that transcend these domain boundaries is what makes for high-flying.

This means using music to think and do mathematics, and using mathematics to think and do music, using science to think and do art, and art to think and do science, using statistics to think and do human rights, and human rights to think and do statistics – these curriculum 'blends' make for a new notion of 'core curriculum'. This is a long way from the way curriculum works as we move up the educational ladder. Instead of broadening and deepening our understanding of the interconnected nature of knowledge, we compartmentalise and fragment knowledge and understanding in ways that disallow the sort of interdisciplinary agility needed for creative thinking and doing. Disciplinary knowledge has its place, and so do specialist fragments of disciplines. However, those fields are not sufficient in themselves to respond to or engage with the super-complex problems we face in times when our templates fail us.

As James Martin, author of *The Meaning of the Twenty-first Century*, makes clear, this is the century of mega-problems all of which have resisted solutions and all of which threaten the planet. He names the following sixteen most intractable problems; that is, those most in need of resolution: global warming; excessive population growth; water shortages; destruction of life in the oceans; mass famine in ill-organised countries; the spread of deserts; pandemics; extreme poverty; growth of shanty cities; unstoppable global migrations; non-state actors with extreme weapons; violent religious extremism; runaway computer intelligence; war that could end civilisation; 'scientific' risks to *Homo sapiens'* existence; a new Dark Age.[17]

No single discipline can 'solve' mega-problems of this sort. They are large, messy and entangled. It is for this reason that governments worldwide are now attempting to advance knowledge-based economy policy models that include some hybridising of the insights of the social sciences, the humanities and science research. At the same time, knowledge researchers are recognising the limits of their conceptualisations and methods and calling for a move beyond interdisciplinarity (that is, using the epistemologies of one discipline within another) to transdisciplinarity (that is, focusing on a social issue both within and beyond disciplinary boundaries).[18] The emphasis on intermediation and embeddedness implies that the creative skills required to be part of meaningful problem-solving efforts are not simply generic but are also context dependent and tightly connected to specific technical and analytic capacities, as well as to social and civic participation.

Creative teams

Just as no single discipline can solve the mega-problems that preoccupy 21st-century scientists and policy-makers, so too the capacities of a single individual are unlikely to be sufficient to build and sustain creative organisations. Creative outputs certainly do depend, to a greater or lesser extent, on the imaginative power of artistic individuals like Ettore Sottsass, at times working alone and in a solitary space. Yet some kinds of creative productivity – for example, scientific breakthroughs – appear to be more reliant on a context of multiple human interactions in a complex social mix. This was true of the environment that allowed Ben to contribute his talents to the creation of the speaker system installed in 2007 at the Queensland Conservatorium of Music.

There is no proven formula for getting the environment right. As creative economist John Howkins points out, patterns of solitary working and group working spring not from one single imperative but from a mix of individuals' inclinations, relevant processes and products, and the social arrangements that pertain to location.[19] Howkins makes a further important point in relation to the social dynamics of the setting in which creative output is optimised:

> When two or more creative people are working in a team, and could not succeed without the team, even to the extent of 'losing' their identity in the team, it is still their personal talent and individual contribution that generates the creativity and the product. It holds both ways. If someone who is part of a team is only part of a team, then they are giving nothing of themselves and they cannot be creative.[20]

As a young creative worker, Ben was part of a dynamic process that involved both his individual smarts and his capacity to work within and for a high-flying and dynamic team with social networks that reached well beyond his own.

Much has, of course, been written about the importance of the team in the contemporary organisation, but less work has been done to describe the characteristics of learning environments that optimise opportunities for students (and, indeed, teachers) to work as members of dynamic creative teams.

This is not to say that 'group work' is unfashionable or that the 'team' has not been the flavour of the month for some time. There is ample anecdotal evidence to suggest that young people have engaged in group work from their earliest years of formal learning and have been brought up on the importance of valuing 'the team'. However, the ambivalence of large numbers of our very capable young people about doing 'group projects' for assessment suggests that their experiences of group work are not, in the main, perceived as likely to add value to the products of their learning; nor has the experience of being in a team in a formal educational setting has necessarily been an enjoyable one. This is so despite all the anecdotal evidence that young people are now highly focused on their relationships and very much plugged in to, and reliant on, their personal social networks.

There are a number of contemporary scholars whose work is helpful in stepping back from romantic notions of both creativity and group work.

Psychologist Mihaly Csikszentmihalyi insists that it is the community, not the individual, that we should focus on to investigate how creativity is fostered.[21] His thesis is quite a complex one, because it involves two key aspects of the environment in which we live and work; that is, the cultural or symbolic order he calls the 'domain' and the social order he understands to be the 'field'. He sees these two aspects interacting with a third component: namely, how humans interact. It is at the intersection of these interactions that creative enterprise emerges. So it is not just a matter of being in the right place at the right time; the right dynamics also need to work – they don't just happen regardless of the where, who and how of engagement.

Norman Jackson is a researcher who has taken Csikszentmihalyi's ideas further, adapting them to specific field of educational practice such as 'history teaching', drawing attention to all the complexity of the social and cultural environments in which such teaching takes place.[22] Importantly, his research shows that creative capacity-building is not simply about having a strong teacher/student relationship or 'gifted' students who like being together, but about a deeper, more complex set of relationships between the people, the ideas and the opportunities for learning provided by the physical environment.

Management consultant Thomas Stewart adds a further layer of complexity to 'community learning' in drawing attention to the importance of 'emptiness' in the generation of ideas that add value to an organisation.[23] He argues that, without space between one field of expertise and another, there can be no creation, because every space for thinking is already occupied. He is critical of managers who 'try to design for everything', arguing the importance of keeping open the space of not knowing: 'I don't know either; what do you think?' Without space for thinking differently, an organisational leader can soon become deaf to the new and potentially value-adding ideas that arise within and outside their business, and blind to the possibilities for moving ideas around to their organisation's best advantage.

To understand the sort of environment that makes not just for group work or team-based work but for dynamic high-flying teams, we can't simply rely on the motivational power of teachers or organisational leaders, or merely hope that individual genius will emerge of its own volition. We should bear in mind John Howkins' insistence, noted above, that creative productivity requires both the separateness of individual talent and the togetherness of team collaboration, all working as seamlessly as possible within and across processes of production and distribution.

Given that the challenge of setting up a learning environment that fosters such a complex mix of relational dynamics is not a simple matter of ensuring that people feel good about themselves, either individually or collectively, then where to from here?

Boids and voids

There are two areas of research that can be usefully brought together to provide principles on which to build a learning environment for 'high-flying' creatives.

The first is research that synthesises computer animation and biological behaviour to understand how 'birds of a feather flock together'. We know that flocking together allows birds ('boids' are the computer-animated variety) to fly higher and exhibit greater scheduling and routing capabilities than each bird can do alone. The means by which this extra capacity is achieved can tell us a lot about how we might do better in a team environment than we can alone.

The second is the sociological research that inquires into how good ideas are picked up and moved about in organisations; that is, how a novel idea, produced in one specialist cluster, can be transported across 'holes' ('voids') in the organisation to be integrated with the work of different, even unrelated, clusters of specialists.

Insights from these two different domains of research – one focusing on the micro dynamics of a team of a few people, and the other focusing on the macro dynamics of working across teams – can be combined to make a good learning environment for creative high-flying.

We will deal with 'structural holes' – voids – once we have investigated the flocking of bird objects – boids.

Boids

Computer modelling expert Richard Seel's inquiry into the emergence of new patterns of behaviour and forms of engagement in organisations serves as a convenient starting point for investigating the value of computer modelling-meets-biology research for 'growing' dynamic creative teams.[24] Seel draws on recent developments in complexity theory, particularly experiments with computer programs to endorse the idea 'simple interactions between simple agents [can] give rise to surprisingly complex behaviour'.[25] He points to three conditions in particular – connectivity, diversity and rate of information flow – that are shown to be important as a result of computer simulation research and observations of physical systems.

Seel concedes, as do other researchers of human social behaviour, that there is more complexity in human interaction than in other natural systems.[26] Nevertheless, much can still be learnt from 'complexity' research about how to optimise creative team development. According to UK educational researcher Paul Tosey, complexity theory can provide a 'radical and innovative frame for professional educational practice' by drawing on computer modelling of the behaviours of natural systems, in particular by observing and attempting to replicate flocks of birds as 'neighbours' or flockmates.[27] In doing so, we can learn the simple rules of interaction that allow for very complex forms of group engagement.

Computer simulations of bird objects (boids) tell us about the behavioural principles that allow flocks or swarms to perform with greater capacity (such as flying higher and faster and avoiding obstacles more easily) than the capacity of any one flock member allows.[28] One of the myths exploded in engaging with this scholarship is the idea that there are no rules when it comes to creative high-flying and, indeed, that there should be no rules; that is, that the best way for creative students to learn is just for others (including teachers) to get out of their way. Computer simulations of flocking demonstrate that there are behavioural rules that allow single biological entities to operate optimally by forming more complex behaviour as a collective. Of course, you can't develop such simulations without rules. The important issue is the nature of the rules and their operation.

A related and important aspect of nature's team behaviour is that it does not come about as a reaction to 'control and command' from outside.[29] When applied to dynamic team environments, this principle puts paid both to the idea that there are no rules to high-flying and to the idea that having rules means that someone must be in absolute control. The 'enhancing' constraints that make for a sense of collective direction are not imposed by a leader. Leadership, in the sense of heading a flock, changes constantly, and 'command and control' is not the means by this change occurs.

Appropriate 'flocking' behaviour is generated within 'local neighbourhoods' of 'flockmates' through the provision of timely information and the self-management of:

↳ separation – the capacity to steer to avoid crowding others

↳ alignment – the capacity to steer towards the average heading of the local flockmates (that is, an average of where the whole flock appears to be heading)

↳ cohesion – the capacity to steer the move towards the average position of local flockmates.

These deceptively simple capacities are three-dimensional in terms of behaviour in that they are simultaneously focused on member/member, member/external and member/colony orientation.[30]

The creative workforce

The rules for maintaining an optimal ecological assemblage of flockmates can tell us a lot about high-flying learning environments. Each flockmate is aligned with and responsive to those flockmates in their immediate vicinity, as well as being appropriately separate from those same flockmates. This may come as something of a surprise to those who understand 'mass collaboration' as necessarily obliterating or subsuming individual space. In fact, it is best done by respecting and maintaining space.

What we can learn from this is that, while creative teams need to be attuned to the needs and interests of their flockmates in the common project, team-based student self-management functions optimally when it does not interfere with or obstruct others. In Seel's terms, 'too much connectivity ... can inhibit emergence [in that] diversity is excluded and groupthink is a very likely outcome'.[31] This means that, despite the good intentions that often accompany the appointment of a strong group leader, the dynamics that flow from this if and when the strong leader takes over might prove to be more of a hindrance than a help. Put simply, space invaders do not help high-flyers.

While boid research works against our commonly accepted notions of strong leadership, it also reminds us that 'anything goes' is not a practical alternative for building a creativity-enhancing learning environment. The space of optimal ecological assemblage is not a space of anarchy – it works precisely against destructively unpredictable conduct on the part of individual flockmates. The necessary randomness is always systematic, scanning for and reporting information of potential value – it is patterned, not chaotic.

Some embryonic work has already been done to apply these principles derived from non-human biological 'teams' to human teams at work within organisations. According to management expert Ken Thompson, the principle of 'systemic randomness' in bio-team behaviour can and should be applied to organisational teams, by encouraging individuals within them to be systematically involved in random interactivity, constantly on the look out for something interesting pertaining to their shared projects and sharing it in a timely way with the group.[32]

This is an important principle and one that I have experienced as highly valuable in my own work. You will see that I have thanked my flockmates in the acknowledgements for their contribution to our individual and collective thinking, and this continues despite the fact that one is in Canada, one in the UK and one in Singapore. All of us stay on the lookout for material that we think might serve the interests of other members of the team, and together we have been able to move faster and higher, in terms of our learning, than any one of us could alone.

Of course, ours has been a very small team within the very large field of higher education. But our small size allows us to be productive as a learning neighbourhood. This follows Thompson's understanding of the size of units that are normal for human teams. He acknowledges elsewhere that there can be differences between human teams and some biological teams in terms of sheer scale of member numbers, with human teams rarely exceeding fifty in number, and typical large organisations rarely exceeding ten thousand members, while biological 'teams' or colonies can number up to a million or more.[33] He points out that humans 'tend to organise themselves into smaller independently managed sub-units' or, to extrapolate from boid research, various 'local neighbourhoods of flockmates'.[34] This purposive activity has the effect of reducing vulnerability to individual member failure while at the same time generating the sort of 'swarm intelligence' that makes for 'amazing scheduling and routing capabilities'[35] well beyond any individual capacity.

The internet has made it possible to harness such 'swarm intelligence' more powerfully than any technology we have yet seen. Swarming mass collaborations on the internet are shaking up orthodox business operations through enhancing their members' capacity for:

↳ give and take (creating shared distribution computing capacity)

↳ finding needles in haystacks (connecting with other like minds through shared interests rather than personal relationships)

↳ participation through passion (co-inventing with others on the basis of shared passion rather than focusing only on profit as motivation).[36]

The creative workforce

Swarming mass collaborations can teach us more about setting up and sustaining high-flying formal learning environments. While there has been much interest and investment in ICT for learning, we have made scant headway in understanding what sorts of collaboration are now possible, and whether and how they might be systematically fostered in formal education. In Seel's terminology, we have much more to learn about how ecological settings and pedagogical approaches can be 'tuned' to predispose young people to creative thinking and doing.[37]

Biological research shows us four types or 'degrees' of collaboration in nature that can improve our understanding of how people's behaviour in teams differs from other sorts of interactive behaviour. They are:

- ↪ solo work – members doing the same things at different times
- ↪ crowd work – members doing the same thing at the same time
- ↪ group work – members doing different things at different times (sequential)
- ↪ team work – members doing different things at the same time (concurrent).[38]

This allows more nuanced understandings of collaborative activity than simply speaking of 'teamwork' as though it were a 'one-size-fits-all' set of activities, behaviour or events. It also directs us to think about matters of size and scale. Is there an optimum number of individuals that could be expected to work concurrently (that is, do different things at the same time) while maintaining cohesion and alignment? What sort of structure would enable a self-managing 'local neighbourhood' to form and be sustained through its capacity to maintain sufficient separateness and sufficient connectedness across time and space?

Voids

As indicated earlier, the move from bio-ecology to human interactivity is not a simply matter of taking what avian or any other species do and applying it to human behaviour. While this fact does not negate the value of learning from natural systems, it reminds us that we need to know more about optimising learning environments than we can learn from boids if we are to set up principles for organising learning environments within business organisations, as well as within and outside schools and universities.

The social scientific research of Stanislav Dobrev and Ronald Burt is helpful here. Dobrev is helpful because his empirical research into career mobility carefully builds a bridge between the spatial proximity of birds and the sociodemographic behaviour of networks of people pursuing similar careers.[39] He finds that some patterns of human behaviour, such as 'job flocking' (the capacity to follow the career mobility of fellow alumni and 'flock' with them), may be explained through ecological dynamics; that is, that ecological proximity can homogenise behavioural outcomes rather than the other way around.

Put simply, individuals do not have to be connected through interpersonal ties to flock together. They can and do connect as do 'birds of a feather'. Nevertheless he also cautions against using ecological models without placing them alongside other theorising of complex social processes. So we can't simply presume that we will fly higher if we attach ourselves to a high-flying crowd or profession.

Ronald Burt's research can be usefully placed alongside Dobrev's job flocking study.[40] It can also give a macro perspective to add to the behavioural rules that operate to maintain flockmate behaviour within natural systems. Burt seeks to understand the mechanism by which 'brokerage' of creative ideas works to generate social capital within an organisation. In doing so, he provides us with a way of linking the idea of local teams as 'neighbourhoods of flockmates' to the macro structures of organisations, and how they enable or constrain the 'vision advantage' that comes from translating good ideas into real value.[41]

In putting forward his views about 'void' brokerage as a creative act, Burt acknowledges the fact that most organisations have structures of clusters in which people's behaviour, opinion and information tend to be relatively homogenous. He explains that the fact that people tend to focus on activities inside their own cluster creates 'holes' in the information flow between groups – what he calls 'structural holes'.[42]

The creative workforce

Burt is interested in the way opinion leaders can bridge these structural holes within an organisation because, as he sees it, the capacity to bridge clusters brings with it the advantages of early detection and development of potentially rewarding opportunities – what he calls 'information arbitrage'.[43] People whose networks can bridge the structural holes 'are able to see early, see more broadly, and translate information across groups', and this in turn provides them with 'a vision of options otherwise unseen'.[44]

There are, according to Burt, four levels of 'translation' or brokerage through which a person or persons can create value as information arbiter(s). They are, in ascending order:

↪ by making people on both sides of the structural hole aware of interests and difficulties that exist in another cluster

↪ by transferring the best of what is going on by transferring the belief or practice into a language that is accessible to the target cluster

↪ by drawing analogies between clusters that are ostensibly irrelevant to each other, and

↪ by synthesising the beliefs and practices of two clusters so that new beliefs or practices emerge that benefit both clusters.[45]

What these levels of arbitrage draw attention to is not just the importance of the brokering function to value-adding creativity but also the significance that attaches to building and expanding 'boundary-spanning relationships' both within and outside the organisational environment.[46]

When applied to formal educational environments, Burt's framework implies that operating as 'neighbourhoods of flockmates' is only part of the picture of a creativity-enhancing learning environment. At a meta-level, someone is needed who can span structural holes across different domains. This demands that someone has the desire, indeed the expectation, 'to continue to propose ideas' that originate in one place and are taken up in another.[47] Applied to schools and universities, this would see art teachers constantly connecting with science teachers, health teachers on the lookout for new ideas coming from the mathematics department, and law lecturers dropping in to see what the IT people are up to.

Taking a reality check

But is this actually happening? In the organisations that Burt studied, the more likely scenario was that leaders and managers had most of their discussions with a small number of very close colleagues and very few with those outside their narrow field of operations. This means that the potential value of good ideas in most organisations is lost; the distribution of ideas is shut down by 'an inertia model of social convenience'.[48] According to Colin Pidd, business consultant and a former senior executive in both the private and the public sectors, the challenge of 'building a bridge' between leaders is one that remains to be addressed in any significant way among Australian CEOs, many of whom still fail to provide the necessary information or guidance when change is being mooted.[49]

So too in schools and universities, ideas do not usually flow freely across disciplinary clusters. Rather, they stop at the door of a faculty or department, as lecturers retreat to monastic offices and teachers go it alone in their one-to-thirty classrooms. If good ideas are going to be valued in formal educational environments, we need to shake up the monasticism and singularity of teaching and educational leadership.

When we put together the lessons about learning environments that are implicit in the biological boid research and the organisational void research described above, we can derive a set of paradoxical principles for dynamic team-building. In summary, they underline the importance of learning environments in which apparently contrary imperatives exist for evoking optimal creative outcomes, imperatives that co-exist despite their apparent incommensurability. They are bringing together the following:

> ↬ *Connectivity with diversity*: an environment in which it is important for students to be plugged into and mindful of a 'local neighbourhood' and a larger world of potential team members

with similar interests or passions, one that allows members to pursue their passions and to contribute to fast-moving flows of information on behalf of others and themselves.

- *Co-invention/co-creation with separation*: an environment in which the nature, purpose and rules of self-management are understood and internalised, so that members can be both separate from and attentive to those they work with and rely on for their high-flying outcomes. The products of learning are authentic productions of the synergies that exist between the individual member and the team, not merely what is required by external others.

- *Leading and following*: an environment in which all team members share collective responsibility for timely and appropriate leadership, looking over the horizon for relevant information for sharing with others while at the same time following the 'steering' of those close by; that is, exercising 'three-dimensional' attention about the local and global, the present and the future.

- *Enhancing constraints and removal of inhibitors*: an environment that minimises 'command and control' while providing scaffolded opportunities for members to conduct themselves in ways that optimise team (and thereby their own) performance – one in which there are, as Paul Tosey puts it, terms, 'good constraints to action'.[50]

- *Creating holes and bridging holes*: an environment in which the spaces that arise naturally between specialist clusters are being bridged by those leaders, managers and others whose understand and value the importance of broad social networks within and outside the institution or organisation, and who are deeply committed to information brokerage.

Making connections

The above principles are aligned in many important respects with recent theorising of learning as a connection-forming or network-creating process. In looking to boids and voids to provide a conceptual framework for rethinking the dynamics of a creativity-enhancing learning environment, we pay less attention to the sources of information and more attention to processes through which knowledge and information are transferred and translated within and among social groups. In a world in which the capacity to memorise predetermined content is much less important than the capacity to generate knowledge through co-creation, this is a key shift. It has us focused on developing connections, not defending the citadel.

Connectivist theorising moves us on from behaviourist, cognitive or constructivist notions of learning to focus squarely on the ecologies within which learning networks are structured. As learning designer George Siemens sees it, our personal networks are dynamic, capable of organising and adapting in order to allow us to form new connections within what is essentially the 'messy, nebulous, informal, chaotic process' of learning.[51] By implication, the work of a designer of learning environments begins with an acknowledgement that the act of learning is a function controlled by the learner. This means that the environment needs to enable learners to build networks and move among them with confidence and agility.

Information and communication technology has a very important role to play in enabling the development of these personal learning networks. As Siemens puts it:

> Blogs, Wikis and other open, collaborative platforms are reshaping learning as a two-way process. Instead of presenting content/information/knowledge in a linear sequential manner, learners can be provided with a rich array of tools and information sources to use in creating their own learning pathways. The instructor or institution can still ensure that their critical learning needs are achieved by focusing instead on the creation of the knowledge ecology. The links and connections are formed by the learners themselves.[52]

The five paradoxical principles outlined above are highly compatible with this conceptualisation of learning as informal, connection-based and ICT-enhanced networking. They make it possible to imagine a new structure for the learning environment, instead of being anxious about what happens once we begin to make the overdue transition away from regulation and rigidity. The five principles privilege the ability to navigate within and across knowledge domains, and are less concerned with the ability to memorise facts or present information. At a micro level, they allow us to be explicit about the dynamics involved in building and sustaining collaborative and agile teams while, at a macro level, they allow us to pay more attention to brokering ideas, understanding that this is a much more crucial institutional and social dynamic than we have acknowledged to date.

The look of learning

The learning environment is not just social and pedagogical and social – it is also physical. When young people enter a space for learning – whether physical or virtual or a combination of both – they receive strong messages about what their experience of learning is likely to be. If the messages they receive tell them that 'good things happen here', that 'people like me seem to enjoy being here' or that 'there is something special going on here', then they are much more likely to engage with the experiences that the environment affords.

As mentioned earlier, it is a sad comment on the low priority given to education that so few educational buildings and resources in post-welfare countries give positive messages about learning. It is more troubling still that many of the architects designing the built environment of our current schools and universities seem to anticipate that the sort of teaching and learning activities for which they are designing will be the same, by and large, as the activities that they remember from their youth. Even now, with all that we ought to know about the nature of learning, we are seeing millions of dollars being poured into creating cinematic spaces in universities and training colleges, so that hundreds of students will be able to stare at one 'expert' standing at a fixed podium and/or an endless procession of PowerPoint slides.

There are, however, some hopeful signs. A recent OECD report, *Twenty-first Century Learning Environments*, brings together a number of examples of innovation in the design of formal learning environments that are much more appropriate to the sort of engagement that are the markers of informal, networked learning in this century.[53] The report distils the creative design inputs of a range of professional groups – administrators, educators, academics, teachers, architects, engineers and facility planners – providing a snapshot of emergent themes in the design of schools and a number of specific examples taken from across the twenty-two participant countries.

They show evidence of a greater understanding of the new purposes of schooling and the importance of opening up schooling both literally and figuratively as spaces in which multiple forms of engagement are not just possible but also desirable. As noted in the report's foreword:

> A school can be a space centre, equipped with the latest technologies … a vocational training centre … a place where communities gather to receive medical care and other support services, to watch exhibitions, to perform and to play sport … [It can] serve to link communities in isolated areas [while] individual elements of a school such as an eco-garden or a DNA-spiral staircase can be learning tools themselves [and it can] embody the creative vision of students, the practical necessities of teachers and the enthusiasm of communities.[54]

At a time when few social institutions have the capacity to bring local communities of people together as churches, kinship group and extended family rituals once did, much is being asked of formal education, but this makes for interesting new possibilities As with the IKEA anecdotes provided in chapter 1, educational problems can also be turned into educational opportunities. If schools and universities are taking more responsibility for community needs, whether or not they have the resources to do so, this fact presents an opportunity to argue for and promote a different type of school, one in which learners are safe and secure, yet stimulated but attractive, imaginative and diversely populated educational environment.

We know that young people's disposition to learning changes for the better when, instead of having thirty adolescents to one teacher, they find themselves learning beside other adults and children younger than themselves, as they might do at work experience or when simply living in the family or community. Our lockstep system of sorting and grading is an obstacle to this sort of broad social engagement, as are the child protection policies that put educators on red alert against 'stranger danger' either in the physical or the virtual environment.

However, as the OECD report, *Twenty-first Century Learning Environments*, shows, it is possible to open up learning spaces and possibilities without endangering young people. It is also possible to remodel traditional spaces so that they are more learner-friendly in design, to combine new and traditional spaces in such a way as to increase spatial diversity, to add mobile ICT classrooms to increase ICT resources, and to integrate schools and their communities more fully, as Millennium High School in New York has done through its high-flying location on three floors of an office building near Ground Zero.[55]

The right to fly

'High-flying' has been used throughout this chapter in its generally accepted sense of a metaphor for success. However, since 9/11 it has had a more troubling connotation. It reminds us of our global failure to broker key concepts for achieving harmony, including those to do with celebrating cultural diversity, racial tolerance and human rights, and the price that we continue to pay for that failure.

There is, however, some good news for the creative workforce. Where once only a small elite of predominantly Anglo middle-class males could aspire to a lifestyle of global travel, flexible work conditions, career advancement and substantial remuneration, now the opportunities have expanded to include any and all with the right mix of talents and skills in the right place at the right time.

While it would be foolish to suggest that the workplace in the twenty-first century is shaking off all the class, ethnicity or gender discrimination of the past, there are certainly healthy signs in terms of the increasing acceptance that a creative workforce is characterised as much by its inclusiveness and its ethical and aesthetic sensibilities as by its networking, digital and ICT capacity. These same qualities should be mirrored in our learning environments to prepare young people for creative life and work before, during and after their formal education.

8

Measuring up

Pablo Picasso once said: 'Computers are useless – they only give answers.'[1] This bold statement makes enormous problems for the tools we use to evaluate and assess the quality of learning. It gives us pause to think about what we want of young people when we come to see how well they measure up. Do we want them, by and large, to 'give answers'? If we do, then how would we distinguish their capacities from those of a computer? And, more importantly, why would we want them to duplicate a computer? If we want something different, what should it be, and how should we go about getting it?

We know that if we value something in education, then we had better assess it. Once we decide to do this, we will have a huge influence on what is taught and how it is taught. It also has a huge influence on how it is reported to key stakeholders like parents and employers. If it is reported as a number or set of numbers that sort 'sheep from goats', then it becomes highly political and captures the attention of everyone, from preschoolers to pro-vice chancellors.

Assessment is therefore one of the most important influences on learning. It sends a powerful message to students about what is important about their learning. Indeed, for many students assessment does not follow engagement with the curriculum – assessment *is* the curriculum! If it's going to be tested, then it counts, even if it is tiddly winks. It is not so long ago that 'how to bleach calico' was an assessable item in home economics! The issue was not that it was relevant – it was taught because it was assessed!

Once we decide that something is not sufficiently 'core business' to be formally assessed, we condemn it to the margins as extracurricular activity. We may still claim to value it, but students see through this very quickly indeed. At a time when so many young adults are doing part-time work as well as study, they are less likely than ever to read widely and ponder questions that are 'outside' what might be tested. Whatever noble aspirations teachers may have to engage young adults in broad-ranging inquiry and deeply analytical discussions, 'the test' is a much more powerful influence on decisions about what they will engage with, how and when. Put bluntly, if it is not likely to be examined, then why bother?

Assessing 'creative capacity', therefore, presents a problem and an opportunity. It is a problem if we see creativity as outside the core; it is an opportunity if and when we engage with creativity as core.

Credible evidence

There can be no credible assessment of creativity unless there is sufficient agreement about what creativity is, so that we know precisely what we are seeking to evaluate and at what stage in the learning process this is best done. This means that we need to clarify whether we are talking about creativity as an idea, as a developmental process or as a product. In other words, are we seeking to assess creative ability as the capacity to conceptualise, the capacity to develop an idea once it has been made familiar, or the ability to produce a final original and high-quality product, or to transport a creative idea, process or product to an unfamiliar place, or all of these? Can we merely infer from the product the extent of creative capacity used in the process of its creation, or can we be more precise, thereby providing credible evidence of the sort used by accreditation and quality assurance agencies to sort and select for education and industry?

There has been a long history of attempts to achieve consensus about what the 'object' of creativity assessment is, and an equally long debate about whether or not consensus is emerging.[2] More than a decade ago, 'creativity researchers' John Feldhusen and Ban Eng Goh were less than sanguine about the possibility of a consensus, saying: 'It is not yet clear that insights derived from very highly creative individuals who have achieved world class recognition for their creativity activity, performance or products will generalise to the lower level of creative or adaptive behavior of people in general or youth in particular. This is a perennial and ubiquitous problem in all psychological and sociological research.'[3]

There was, however, as these authors indicate, a breakthrough of sorts in the 1990s. This came with the insistence of Teresa Amabile and Mihaly Csikszentmihalyi that creativity is better understood as a process that occurs outside an individual rather than a mysterious individual capacity.[4] Once creativity is 'exteriorised', it becomes possible for independent observers to agree that what they are observing is or is not creative. And once creativity can be systematically observed over time, criteria can be established for formalising such systematic observations into an evaluation strategy or regime of assessment.

The conclusion that Feldusen and Ban Eng Goh drew from their extensive study of the research done before the mid-1990s is unsurprising. They concluded that creativity is multidimensional, requiring therefore multiple channels of measurement such as inventories and tests that measure everything from individual 'cognitive processes, motivations interests, attitudes and styles' to 'the products, presentations and performances' that result from creative processes.[5] This moves us away, thankfully, from the temptation to conflate 'creative' with 'gifted and talented', the latter category being unhelpful in thinking of creativity as everyone's business.

UK educator Anna Craft has pursued lines of inquiry that continue this trend away from assessing creativity as individuality and exceptionality.[6] Craft provides a firm demonstration of just how much the focus of creativity research has been democratised. She insists that we are now working in a different 'climate' of engagement with creative capacity, a climate characterised by a new breadth of emphasis on:

↪ ordinary creativity rather than genius

↪ characterising rather than measuring

↪ the social system rather than the individual

↪ encompassing views of creativity that include products but do not see these as necessary.[7]

In speaking of 'characterising' creativity rather than measuring it, Craft draws attention to a real dilemma for the assessment and/or evaluation of creativity: how do we provide credible evidence of creative capacity? Put in the more complex and clunky language of educational assessment, how do we develop, analyse and integrate multiple types of evidence at different levels of scale and scope, so that the dynamic and situated nature of creative capacity in action can be captured in authentic and meaningful ways? Having done so, how do we express this in a language that is widely understood among stakeholder groups?

The idea that creativity may be assessable through a multiplicity of instruments is the good news and bad news for educators, just as it is for employers who want formal educational reporting to tell them precisely what potential employees can do as 'creatives'. There is widespread agreement that no single tick-a-box test can do this, nor can a one-off intelligence test. And this is, in essence, why the rubber of creative capacity has yet to meet the road of formal assessment. It's very hard to do.

Cold calculation

While it is not necessary or desirable here to elaborate on the historical development of theories about what makes assessment credible, it is important to indicate that there has been, particularly since the 1950s, a powerful tradition for theorising credibility in terms of the validity of educational measurement. It is a tradition that ties assessment to the measurement of phenomena through laws that allow generalisable explanation or prediction.[8]

The core business of this tradition is to offer principles, practices and types of evidence through which credibility is established through test scores and their interpretation. As a discipline, it questions any approach that assessment developers and users might adopt if it falls outside this logic of validity. Test scores are used to make comparisons between like others, and this makes them important for educational authorities and policy-makers who want to know how individuals and groups compare when ranked in terms of a particular skill – say, literacy or numeracy. This ranking provides a rationale for funding certain projects and refusing or cutting funding to others.

We should not underestimate the powerful hold of this tradition on educational assessment and, in particular, the power it has to weaken the credibility of 'alternative' approaches by marginalising them as 'cases where the common interpretation and validity inquiry do not hold'.[9] Writing about the power of this tradition to frustrate attempts to assess creativity as original conceptualisation, Rob Cowdroy and Erik de Graff are pessimistic in terms of the possibility of assessing creativity at all: 'Pressures for conformity with conventions of assessment in other fields of education, and reinforced by global quality assurance demands for objectivity, uniform standards and transparency reinforce focus of assessment on the demonstrable execution and the tangible product and preclude assessment of creative ability.'[10]

Yet while we must confront the misalignment of our assessment conventions with creativity in the sense of ideational power, we should not overestimate the credibility of these same conventions with the larger community of stakeholders who have become increasingly sceptical of coldly calculated 'test scores' and what they mean. As indicated in chapter 3, the growing trend among many employers is to see whether the credential box is ticked, then get down to the real business of seeing what attributes their graduates actually have, rather than to interpret a high grade credential as high employability. Put simply, we do have growing consensus that credibility means more than 'validity'.

The creative workforce

Achieving consensus

If we are to crack the tough nut of making assessment of creativity credible, then consensus is needed around creativity as a process or set of processes that are amenable to systematic observation. In the UK, the Imaginative Curriculum Project revealed a fairly consistent reiteration of five positive ideas most associated with creativity among the academics surveyed. They were:

↪ being imaginative
↪ being original
↪ exploring for the purpose of discovery
↪ using and combining thinking skills
↪ communicating as an integral part of the creative process.[11]

Importantly, the UK academics in the sample disagreed with the proposition that creativity is a rare individual gift. In Australia, a recent survey of academics' attitudes to creativity based on the UK study found, likewise, that their understandings of creativity were more closely tied to thinking and problem-solving skills, self-discipline and work ethic, than to individual genius.[12] Both groups of academics predominantly perceived the concept of creativity as seeing unusual connections and having imagination and original ideas. The notion of creativity as a 'mysterious process' was the lowest ranked item for both sample populations.

While these findings point to more definitional clarity than we have seen to date, little seems to have changed when it comes to assessing creative capacity in universities, if the student participants in the UK study are any guide. This is how a number of them depict their experiences:

> Having exams, for goodness sake, it makes me so mad that we have to go into an exam and give them back what they have given us in a year of lectures … You just regurgitate information. Waste of time.[13]

> If you've got [a teacher] who's quite dogmatic or only interested in basing things on an evidence and research basis, [creativity] is just not going to happen.[14]

> It's also about spontaneity, isn't it? So you can be creative and you've spent a month revising and your head is full of crap.[15]

It should not be presumed that students are the only ones frustrated by the dominant transmission model of content delivery and assessment. The Australian study found that many of the award-winning academic teachers surveyed were highly critical of the ways in which creativity and their attempts to assess it were shut down by the policies and procedures of their institution.[16] When asked to comment on what they perceived to be the major inhibitors to fostering creativity in their students, they named the following as obstacles:

- ↪ 'Multiple choice examination, large classes and lack of available academic time to mentor and provide meaningful feedback to students are major inhibitions. In the sciences, academics who try and impose a specific learning strategy or worldview on their students are often stifling creativity, as are those who are unwilling to alter 'traditional' assessment formats.'

- ↪ 'Exams!'

- ↪ 'Lecturers who teach students to follow a recipe. Exams.'

- ↪ 'Didactic, content driven and controlled processes that deny students the opportunity for intellectual exploration and experimentation with ideas.'

- ↪ 'Large classes; multiple choice testing; lack of challenging, creative assessments (due to marking required).'

- ↪ 'The whole paradigm of objectivist teaching learning and assessment, in particular:
  - the subject-centred, expert-driven, transmission-of-information model of university teaching and assessment
  - the passive, dependent, competitive, non-reflective learning prevalent among our students
  - the clinical supervision model of the practicum/internships in professionally oriented courses.'

- ↪ 'Exams!'

- ↪ 'Inflexible curricula. Over-prescribed learning outcomes. Over-specific assessment tasks and criteria (and exams!).'[17]

We may have more work to do to establish what counts as creativity, but we certainly seem to have reached consensus about its nemesis. The enemy is the exam!

As one of the surveyed academics makes clear, however, exams are merely one technique in a larger set of techniques that make up a coherent cultural climate, what the respondent calls 'the whole paradigm of objectivist teaching, learning and assessment'. In this climate, 'the subject-centred, expert-driven, transmission-of-information model of university teaching and assessment' is the orthodoxy, whereas assessing creative capacity is an alternative idea, an experiment on the fringe of the mainstream. The fact of examining is not the enemy: the enemy is the narrowness of what counts as credible examining in the prevailing climate.

In terms of teaching and assessing, creativity may be 'not yet', but the rhetoric of creativity is ubiquitous. A recent analysis of higher education policy documents in Australia indicates that 75 per cent of Australian universities have an expressed commitment to 'creative' learning outcomes.[18] As Norman Jackson puts it, the problem in universities worldwide is 'not that creativity is absent but that it is omnipresent'.[19] Yet he also notes, ironically, that it is 'rarely an explicit objective of the learning and assessment process'.[20] While a lot of lip service is paid to such 'alternative' techniques in progressive policy documents, and while teaching awards may throw a shaft of light on these hidden corners of activity, the weight of eight hundred years of didactic and mimetic traditions of learning is not so easily thrown off.

Who assesses whom?

Is it fair to blame the weight of tradition for our inability to embrace creativity as a driver of pedagogy, curriculum and assessment? Historical inquiry into universities shows that our pedagogical traditions may not be as long or as coherent as we have come to think. In fact, we have lost a number of traditions that might make for a very different sort of campus (and perhaps a much more interesting one!) than is the norm today.

On medieval campuses, teaching guilds set rigorous standards for the conduct of pedagogical work and for admission to the profession of teaching, a precarious occupation in which a 'living' was dependent upon an academic's capacity to attract and hold students. A 'junior lecturer' ('batchelor') often paid students to assess 'him' (rather than the other way around) by 'attend[ing] his lectures and criticis[ing] him so that he might see and rectify his mistakes'.[21] This put academics under very high pressure to be personally and professionally accountable for their teaching, more so than they are now, notwithstanding the 'audit explosion' we are now experiencing across the entire educational sector.[22]

The great academic teacher Peter Abelard assessed the pedagogical practices of his ageing mentor, William of Champeaux, as well below par:

> I was at first welcomed but later cordially disliked, when I tried to refute some of his opinions and ... argued against him and sometimes seemed superior in disputation ... I a mere youth, conspired to conduct classes ... with what envy our Master began to grow green ... For one that had earlier had some students, such as they were ... he lost them all and was so compelled to give up teaching ... [He was an] old man for whom long practice rather than ingenuity had made a name. To whom if anyone went uncertain as to any question, he came away more puzzled. He was indeed a wonder in the eyes of his auditors but of no account in the sight of those who asked him questions. He had a wonderful command of language but contemptible sense and no reasoning power. When he lit the fire, he filled the house with smoke, not with light.[23]

While envy and suspicion of youthfulness may well be seen to be the unfortunate but understandable product of an ageing ego, other allusions in Abelard's reflection speak quite directly to the matter of teaching quality. 'Losing all one's students' was as stark and authentic an assessment of poor teaching quality as we might imagine. Then, as now, students were attracted to rigour and energy, and eschewed pomp and tediousness.

What is also worth remarking on is the extent to which the creative capacities of a youthful and talented student were disconcerting for a senior academic unused to being intellectually challenged from 'below'. We can imagine the satisfaction that a precocious Abelard had

The creative workforce

in making that challenge, and we can also see the clarity with which such a perceptive young student saw through the limitations of his ageing teacher, assessing his performance as less than credible. If there is an equally perennial tradition to didacticism and imitation, it is the sceptical student's assessment of their teacher's performance!

The medieval tradition of academics paying students for assessment is one that we are very unlikely to see revived in our 'enlightened' times. Students do give feedback, of course, but it can be manipulated or ignored for a host of reasons. However, the medieval tradition reminds us that authentic assessment does not have to be a one-way process. If we come to understand effective 21st-century teaching as less about being a Sage-on-the-Stage and more about being a Meddler-in-the-Middle, as argued in chapter 4, then we are compelled to ask 'Who assesses whom?' without having a simple and obvious answer.

When teachers and students are repositioned as project partners, as co-directors and co-editors of their social world, who then is the rightful assessor of the value of that cultural assemblage: the teacher, the student, an external 'other' or all of these? The work is no longer clean of all sets of fingerprints, but is tainted by co-direction and co-editorship at every level. So what does it mean to make judgments to credential individuals on the basis of the quality of the co-creation? And what new dilemmas are set up around 'objective' assessment?

Once we begin to open up the possibility that teachers may not be the only credible assessors – or that teachers might even be implicated in what is being assessed – we open a can of worms for the measurement of student performance. This is because of the inevitable tension that exists between the democratic classroom as an ideological ideal and the role of formal educational institutions as sorters, credentiallers and reporters to industry and the professions. Experiments that involve more than one assessor and move away from top-down assessment have long languished on the fringes of education: J. S. Neill's Summerhill was never likely to become every future employer's dream!

It is needs to be said here that, despite all the scepticism they may bring to their evaluation of an individual teacher's performance, the students themselves – especially the high achievers among them – are a force for conservatism in the assessment game. As products of the measurement culture, they are very likely to resist any apparent move to 'downgrade' the quality assurance that 'objective' assessment seems to provide. Students understandably share with many in the community a belief that, in its purest form, 'democratic assessment' is oxymoronic. The Yuk/Wow Generation may be quicker than ever to question a low grade, but it does not necessarily follow that they want to substitute alternative forms of bottom-up assessment for traditional top-down ones.

Example 8.1 elaborates how one university lecturer whom I supervised to a successful doctorate wrestled with the issue of democratising assessment as he sought to make for a more authentic evaluation of his students' creative processes and products than he felt he could do alone from 'above'. It is a useful demonstration of the construction of a 'differently coherent' cultural climate in which creativity-friendly assessment strategies can flourish.

Example 8.1 Peer-to-peer assessment

Don Lebler, a lecturer in popular music at the Queensland Conservatorium of Music, is one university teacher who has worked extremely hard to overcome the barriers to peer assessment that derive from student and staff expectations that 'transmission' pedagogy will be the norm in his classes. 'You're the experts,' he tells his students. 'This is your music so you're better placed to assess its quality than your teachers are.'

By the time they enter his course at the conservatorium, his talented students have already developed quite sophisticated ways of self-monitoring the standard of their performances. More than three-quarters of them belonged to bands outside school, and this has played a key role in their musical development. They have come to rely on feedback from bandmates, audiences, friends and audio recording more than on teacher feedback.

Lebler believes that the prior learning behaviour of these students provides a strong foundation for inducting them into the Bachelor of Popular Music as a self-directed learning program. In 2005, he set up a process of assessment that was aligned with the ethos of self-direction he embedded in the entire program. This involved the students in providing systematic feedback to each other, both informally through written responses to songs and other creative works, and formally through a discussion board that also made an assessment of the quality of work done. The board consisted of students and teachers, with students being in the majority.

Not only did Lebler's students receive much more authentic feedback on their work than he or his baby boomer colleagues were able to give alone but also they received it in a more timely way than one lecturer could do with a cohort of twenty or so students. Interestingly enough, the end-of-semester results for the cohort were not significantly different in terms of past grade profiles, so the fears held by staff and others that the students might collectively inflate their results proved to be unfounded.

The students very much appreciated the diversity of musical styles that was made available to them during the process. One student wrote: 'I was amazed at the variety of genres present, and saw some students taking some strong creative risks that proved very successful with the listeners', while another student commented: 'My writing and playing style has been greatly influenced and changed over these last few months through all the live music I have seen and through the fellow musicians I have been working with.'

Importantly, many of his students came to value collaboration in the creative act, instead of simply competing with one another: 'Collaboration has been a large part in making this an enjoyable experience for me. I found that working with other people has not only sharpened me as a musician but it has also helped me as a person.'

Lebler's 'real' peer-to-peer assessment was a success in a number of ways:

↪ It provided useful feedback to a majority of the students who presented work, while at the same time increasing their awareness of the range of music that was currently being developed by their peers – who was doing what and how. This made co-creation much more likely than it had previously been.

↪ It inducted students into using the electronic communication system through the course website. This prepared them for making their major study submissions similarly at the end of semester.

↪ It gave students the experience of providing feedback, including an understanding of what kinds of feedback their peers regarded as acceptable.

↪ As individual students became used to the innovative assessment practices of the course, the gap between self-assessed marks and those awarded by the assessment panels narrowed with that experience.

The last point mentioned in example 8.1 is a very important one, in light of what has been said in earlier chapters about the importance of judicious self-criticism as an attribute of 'creatives'. The peer-to-peer assessment practices are not only useful for evaluating how the students' work measures up in a broader context of opinion than academics alone can provide; they are also a means for individual students to learn how to judge their own performance in relation to those of their peers. In this way, the tendency of individual students to be either overly self-critical or self-congratulatory can be modified. Armed with this experience of how to conduct their own reality check, these students are well placed to be part of a workplace that values not only a team ethic but also a capacity for providing highly credible self- and peer-based evaluations of the quality of their processes and products.

It is not just in Lebler's program that students have been found to receive more meaningful feedback from their peers than they do from their teachers. This was also found in a study of self- and peer assessment conducted at Mount Sinai School of Medicine in New York.[24] Students were better able to review their own progress as a result of peer feedback than they were when reliant on teacher feedback alone.

The amount of credibility that can or ought to be given to self-review is, of course, a tricky issue. One the one hand, we know that the capacity to take responsibility for authentic self-appraisal, like the capacity to learn from error-making, is one of the attributes that young people need to engage in 'value-added' thinking and doing. As one of the generic skills of personal development, it remains suspect as a quality too easily manipulated or misrecognised, in much the same way that personal memories of youthful experiences are suspect for the possibility that they may be strongly held but false.

So is it impossible to bring together the 'personal' and the 'assessable'? Medical educator Susan Toohey argues to the contrary.[25] However, she also cautions that personal development is not measurable using traditional test instruments. Example 8.2 is a distillation of her description of the development and judicious use of personal portfolios as a means for students to take responsibility for their learning and assessment of that learning.

Example 8.2 Self-assessment

At the medical faculty of the University of New South Wales, Susan Toohey and her colleagues wanted to prepare medical practitioners so that they were 'prepared to look carefully and analytically at their own mistakes', able to 'co-operate, rather than engage in destructive competition' and were 'prepared to acknowledge when they have reached the limits of their skills and call in a second opinion rather than push on regardless'.

To this end, they set up a regime of assessment that went beyond examinations and assignments to evaluate those outcomes that they regarded as highly desirable in terms of professional behaviour but not amenable to 'competency' testing. They saw these as the personal qualities and dispositions that cannot be 'mastered' at any time but are always open to improvement.

There were two key drivers of the thinking Toohey and her colleagues did about assessment. The first was that assessment should be geared to 'improvability', not competency, and the second was that relevant assessment instruments would need to be found that, when taken together, would provide a 'portfolio' of evidence of personal growth in relation to the qualities that are highly valued by medical colleagues.

They considered a range of assessment items for this purpose, including:

↪ *Assessment of personal insight and self-management*, using a combination of team review and self-assessment methods, all of which is jointly reviewed by each individual student at a meeting with their 'clerkship director'. Entries kept in learning diaries and journals also feed into this process. The students access 'a prescribed format' for the learning diary, which is 'kept as an electronic document in a Microsoft Access database'.

↪ *Assessment of self-directed learning*, using individual learning contracts for elective study modules that broaden the tasks students undertake as they progress through the learning program. The tasks begin narrowly in the first year with academic skills, such as conducting a literature review, but broaden in the following years to include making contact with and interviewing people, public speaking and so on.

↪ *Assessment of communication and teamwork*, using assessment by simulated or 'standardised' patients with whom the practitioner is observed interacting. These standardised patients (actors or former patients) are trained to assess the empathy they experience emanating from the practitioner in that engagement, with students who lack this quality being directed to programs designed to help them

remediate this deficit. This can be augmented by a tutor's assessment
of teamwork skills displayed in the group work undertaken for a 'triple
jump examination' and assessment by team members as colleagues
or peers.

Convinced by the evidence that personal development can and should be
assessed, the faculty made a decision that students would present a portfolio that included peer assessment, negotiated learning contracts and
reflective writing as part of their overall program, to be assessed in every
second year of the six-year program. In this way, they 'allow students to
develop their own understanding of the personal attributes and evaluate
their own progress while offering opportunities for regular feedback from
professional and academic colleagues'.

The personal portfolio is not something that only adults can use. It
is a very valuable instrument for assessment as learning in the hands
of all students when support and direction is given about its purposes
and processes. Attention must be given to it as a dynamic documenta-
tion process, not a CV, if it is to be used optimally for learning and its
assessment. This will not happen if the pedagogical processes around
the portfolio are undeveloped. It will collapse into a repository, of no
more or less use than a filing cabinet.

Portfolios do not contain the evidence as much as point to the evidence. They are usually structured as edited assemblages of 'snapshots'
or instances in an iterative process of learning and performing. The
processes of portfolio compilation allow people of every age to take
responsibility for their learning, through developing a meta-language
for explaining their own learning journey and what they are able to
perform as an outcome of that learning. The structure of a portfolio
works as a scaffolding for the development of that language.

It is through this meta-language that claims about individual
capacities are made and warranted. The claims and warrants are made
credible through taking a relevant selection of instances in the process
and making it intelligible as evidence to an external audience. Through
this process, young people learn to make judgments about which claims
are relevant to which capacities and how they would warrant these in

their own individual case. So they would learn how to customise their selection of snapshots or instances, depending on the attributes being sought. They would then be able to take full responsibility for selecting the material for warranting a claim they might make about their personal qualities, for example, a claim to be flexible in their approach, or empathic, or a good team worker.

An electronic portfolio can used by any student to bring together a synthesis of their academic results, work experience, community and personal skills for easy access by employers and for on-going assembling and editing according to their professional and personal needs. E-portfolios can be customised to serve as *curriculum vitae*, but their potential is much greater than that. They can, if thoughtfully assembled, allow the fullness of a skills acquisition and learning journey to be made explicit, not just relevant examination or standardised test results.

A strongly developed capacity to cut and paste an assemblage to suit a particular employment opportunity is a very desirable outcome of this process. No employer is likely to have the time or the inclination to wade through a treatise or personal diary. The skills developed during the portfolio development process allow a young person to cut to the chase by tailoring a version of the portfolio to the specifics of a project role. This can be done as many times as is necessary to a 'portfolio career'.

A portfolio need not encompass years of learning; it may be useful as a working document that grows dynamically within a short-term activity. Researchers at Goldsmiths College, London, utilised a short-term portfolio – what they called an 'unpickled portfolio' – when trialling various forms of 'authentic' assessment of design and technology capacities of young adolescents.[26]

Assigned by the Assessment of Performance Unit of the UK's Department of Education and Science to develop an innovative approach to the assessment of design capacities, Kay Stables and Richard Kimbell developed models of assessment that made explicit the way task-focused creative thinking occurs in the context of an explicit design task and how such thinking can be further enabled through strategic use of evidence prompts. Example 8.3 is a distillation of one of their published papers in which they set out the details of their innovative approach.

Example 8.3 Assessing design innovation

The challenge faced by Stables and Kimbell was 'to assess the design and technological capabilities of a 2 per cent sample of the 15-year-old population of England, Wales and Northern Ireland (about 10,000 learners)'. They were challenged to develop assessment that would provide credible evidence, but would also be able to be conducted as pen and paper tests in the relatively short timeframes that are typically used by teachers for assessing high school students.

They approached the matter of eliciting evidence by conceptualising assessment as having a three-fold purpose:

↪ to expose capability to the scrutiny of assessors
↪ to enable the learner to 'see' the evidence for themselves in such a way as to encourage learners to 'modify and enrich the product they are working on', and
↪ to maximise the learner's ability to make their thinking explicit, thereby 'improving their more generic designing processes'.

In the first trial, the researchers created a scenario that was the design challenge for the students: a local community taking over a wasteland to utilise it for community purposes. They found that the students remained enthusiastically on task, but the researchers felt that they did not have sufficient evidence of the thought that was accompanying the design decisions the students were making.

In the next trial they interrupted the students every ten minutes, an 'annoying and valuable' strategy that allowed students to reveal their thinking. They further refined this approach into a structured unfolding booklet – the 'unpickled portfolio' – which allowed the interaction of thinking and doing to be made explicit not just to the assessors but also to the students. They were able to document how students' thinking moved from 'hazy impressions – imaging and modelling inside the head' through speculating and exploring, clarifying and validating and critically appraising, at the same time as students' doing moved from 'confronting reality outside the head' to initial drawings, diagrams, notes, graphs and numbers, then to modelling in solid materials to predict or represent reality, then to prototyping or provisional solutions.

The structured unfolding booklet was an important departure from the traditional examination booklet. When combined with photographs of the evolving work and voice files about the thinking behind the work, it worked as a portfolio that allowed students and assessors to see a 'snap-shot story-line of the route that learners took to their prototype solution', as well as having a positive effect on the performance of the learners in terms of their anticipation of tasks and their growing confidence. With photographic evidence as a reality check, students became 'less "precious" about preserving the models themselves'.

Example 8.3 is important to creative capacity-building for a range of reasons, not the least of which is that it interrogates thinking and doing as interactive processes, rather than understanding doing as simply the outcome of a prior process of thinking. The protocol based on 'concurrent verbalisation' of evidence worked as a spur to development as well as being authentic evidence of actual development. The overall process was popular with students in a way that most examinations are not; it was not simply another 'test' but also an authentic learning experience and a creative opportunity.

A further strength of the assessment process is the extent to which it encouraged judicious self-criticism once the process was elaborated to include photos and voice files. In light of issues raised in chapter 6 about 'preciousness' as an obstacle to creativity, this is a bonus. It means that students can and do take more responsibility for their output than when they are trying to guess what is in the mind of the teacher.

The success of the Stables and Kimbell trials has been an important step forward in the difficult work of authenticating assessment of creativity, by showing how schemata under development can be systematically addressed from the very beginning of the thinking and doing process. This is very important if there is to be any acknowledgement of the concept on which a particular product or creative work is based.

And there should be, according to academics Rob Cowdroy and Erik de Graff. These two researchers try to tackle the most difficult problem of providing authentic assessment for creative works as quantum-generating research in universities. There is a lot at stake in this quest, because it can mean the rise or fall of whole faculties that are able or unable to make the case that their creative output should count as research.

Cowdroy and Graff propose that authentic assessment of creative capability needs to address the relationship between concept, schema, craft and product, by interrogating what they call the 'line of flight' from concept to actualisation.[27] But they do more than stress the importance of taking into account the various stages of creative endeavour that leads to a product. They also provide examples of what they call the 'Authenticative Assessment' model for evaluating the three stages they identify with creativity as a learning outcome: conceptualisation, schematisation and execution. A summary of this model is provided in example 8.4.

Example 8.4 Authenticative assessment

'Authenticative assessment' is a scholarly approach to evaluation of creative work that moves the focus from the work itself as a product or outcome to 'the conceptual and schematic underpinnings of the work as articulated by the author'. It is understood to be most relevant to the context of higher education, where it is presumed that 'creators' are able to 'present and defend' their creative process in either an oral or a written format.

The assumptions on which the approach is based are:
- that creative works cannot speak for themselves
- that teachers cannot directly assess conceptualisation or schematisation because of their cerebral, abstract and invisible nature
- that teachers can assess a student's understanding of conceptualisation or schematisation, in terms of relevant theoretical and philosophical frameworks
- that student articulation needs to be done through the shared language provided by particular philosophical and conceptual frameworks
- that students' articulating their originating concepts in this way is a means of authenticating the process of creative development to the point of execution of the completed work.

This approach to assessing creative capacity evaluates the worth of the work in terms of the process of its production, and this includes the theoretical ideas and models that have informed it before the work took physi-

The creative workforce

cal shape. The approach was trialled in Urbino, Italy, and in Drama, Greece, in the mid-1990s. A more recent full-scale application was undertaken in the Bachelor of Architecture program at the University of Newcastle, Australia, where student grades 'are based on evidence [from the student's presentation and defence] of the clarity and consistency of intellectual development of a conceptual idea through schematization and execution to the completed work'.

The Authenticative Assessment model can be used to respond to demands in the higher education sector for authenticating artistic works as research. It is an approach that will be somewhat familiar to those whose doctoral studies have required them to write a thesis and provide an oral defence of that thesis in the shared language of disciplinary scholarship. The matter of the quantity of evidence needed for the purposes of authentication would need to be judged according to the size of the project and the year level of the student.

While Cowdroy and Graff do not include the transporting of ideas across 'structural holes' in their understanding of the stages of the creative process that ought to be assessed, they nevertheless move us on to link assessment and artistic production in a way that respects both.

Speaking digitally

There are synergies between the Authenticative Assessment model described in example 8.4 and John Seely Brown's more general call for a shared language through which it is possible to speak meaningfully about processes of creative cultural production. Both are interested in the role language plays in communicating the what and how of creativity. Seely Brown advocates a vernacular for 'speaking' the student's ability to cut and paste words, images, sounds, artefacts and ideas in new and meaningful ways – to store, apply and then discard them when no longer useful.[28] And, like Cowdroy and de Graff, Seely Brown stresses the need to probe the way individuals think about the processes they are employing to address complex problems, including their ability to critically evaluate the efficacy of their strategies, and to engage peers in that process of critical evaluation.

However, Seely Brown is less sanguine about the relevance of the current disciplinary languages and conceptual frameworks for this purpose. He stresses the importance of using a 'digital vernacular' as 'a new kind of language, which includes understanding how graphics, colour, lines, music and words combine to convey meaning'.[29] Our current narrowly word-centric and discipline-centric assessment practices are simply not adequate to this task.

The powerful influence of digital tools on academic literacies, and thus on their evaluation, is undeniable. We have seen, among other things, a shift from input to output brought about through the shift from handwriting to electronic writing. The speed with which we can not only type using a keyboard but also edit to produce a final 'clean' copy accelerates the entire process of text production, giving us less time for reflection than was allowed by the pen-and-ink process. This is not to argue that the quality of the texts we produce electronically is any better or worse in the long run. The point is that many of our purposes for producing texts – and the ways we produce them – have now changed quite radically. Our assessment tools have rarely followed suit.

Because non-linear, non-sequential thought is becoming more valuable than traditional linear cumulative argument, we needing more 'grabs', 'sound bites' and link-friendly hypertext for the fast-paced entrepreneurial world in which most of us have time neither to write nor to read long-hand prose. Indeed, many young people can now no longer read 'running writing', and this is creating a problem for novice researchers who need to read handwritten archival records. The fact that we still require handwriting overwhelmingly for doing exams is an anachronism of the first order.

We are also seeing the combination of 'image–text–sound' as simultaneous elements, not simply one as garnish to the others. Now that we have ways to play with text, and new ways to assemble and edit information, we are less likely to have the time or inclination to turn the pages of *Encyclopaedia Britannica* and more likely to access Wikipedia. In summary, because creative 'linking' is now such an important part of creative thinking and doing, editorial, navigational and communication capacities need to be included in every 'pre-professional' assessment regime. Leaving it all to computing or communication studies simply won't do.

Many 'creative' workers will find themselves working in the digital content sectors where they will be required to do more than articulate the conceptualisation, schematisation and execution of their creative outputs. They are likely to have a risk-taking and innovative mindsets, an integrative problem-solving ability, a high level of technical knowledge and applications ability, and entrepreneurial business acumen.

As elaborated earlier, they will be able to manage a portfolio career, as a self-employed, freelance, casual or part-time worker, and not necessarily with a single employer or in a single industry. Given the project-based nature of much of their work, they will be working in teams with multiple partners who change over time, so they will be culturally and geographically agile. In the fast-moving, highly competitive international environment, as the sustainability and relevance of our economic and social systems will become more complex, they will be constantly updating their skills and capacities, including the skills of project management and entrepreneurship. Life design will be an increasing priority, as they seek to move from entry-level workforce jobs to high-flying destinations.

In digital times, it is the capacity to engage in value-adding assembling and disassembling processes – rather than the ability to memorise and regurgitate content knowledge – that needs to be prioritised in any authentic regime of assessment for creative capacity-building. This capacity is likely to be optimally displayed in groups and cohorts of students co-creating, co-editing and co-evaluating in conjunction with each other and with staff, as in example 8.1, rather than giving the correct answers to questions as an isolated 'answering machine'. In other words, the dominance of individual memorisation assessment needs radical rethinking.

Making judgments about whether a prospective employee will measure up in terms of all the desirable skills and attributes of a 'creative' worker is not simply a matter of accumulating undergraduate degrees in business and information technology as well as a degree in the creative industries or the creative arts. This says something powerful not just about the inadequacy of any one degree or disciplinary field to qualify the creative worker but also about the problem of disciplinary borders in general. Subject content and expertise are not dead by any means, but regurgitating them as information is inadequate to assessing the potential of future creatives, given the short shelf-life of our disciplinary knowledge and the speed with which our technology allows knowledge to be combined.

School meets industry

There is no clear picture of the relationship between educational success and creative capital. Some very successful creatives have been less than impressive or interested in their formal education, while others have thrived both within and beyond their schooling. One thing is sure, however. Given the propensity of the Yuk/Wow Generation to want it all now, it is unlikely that they will be willing or able to linger in any pre-service context for very long. They certainly won't be interested in spending six or more years as a full-time undergraduate in order to get three sets of credentials.

This is where a well-customised portfolio can be very useful, because it can demonstrate a breadth of skills developed over a shorter period than an undergraduate degree generally requires. What the portfolio does, if well constructed, is to provide credible evidence of skills developed in part-time employment and in community leadership and recreation activity. Many of these activities may be much more likely than formal testing to provide credible evidence of creative team outputs in which the individual played a specific role. Well-assembled and well-edited portfolios point to more than what a young person knows and can do; they give a clear indication of how well the person knows it and can do it, and under what conditions.

As indicated earlier, it is a rare – and naive – employer who confidently assumes that they will learn all they need to know about the capacities of a potential employee by looking at their formal credentials. So employers have much to gain from the trend to the more integrated approach to assessment in which the self-managing learner takes responsibility for the assemblage or collage of evidence of their capability.

This does not, of course, mean that employers can or should abrogate their rights and responsibilities to apply their preferred assessment instruments to gauge employment skills and attributes. A raft of tools is now available for this purpose, some of which test specific technical skills that pertain to an employment role, while others test generic capacities and/or personal attributes.

Internationally, there is widespread employer support for generic skills testing instruments, particularly those that allow for contextualisation of the generic skill to the discipline or professional area. However, a recent survey has shown that generic tools currently in use – for example, the Graduate Skills Assessment (GSA) and the Employability Skills Profiler (ESP) – are being rejected by universities as either too costly (as is the case with the GSA) or too generic to be of value (as with the ESP).[30] Moreover, academics have been critical of the written or online instruments used to assess practical and interpersonal skills.

In broad terms, the trend in assessment for employment is towards utilising a variety of instruments that are not just dependent on school, university or technical college results, including observation in various settings, simulated group work, oral presentations, written responses to scenarios, and performance during an interview, as well as a host of psychometric aptitude or personality tests. Industry-based assessment is therefore becoming a more time-consuming and costly process, with small and medium enterprises being particularly disadvantaged because they are less likely to use assessment centres or to have dedicated selection and recruitment personnel.[31]

Because many 'creatives' will be self-employed or working in small to medium businesses, the trend to self-managed performance review and assessment is mutually beneficial. With student-managed e-portfolios becoming more acceptable to business and universities as 'a practical method for graduates to explain and provide examples of their employability skills',[32] new opportunities exist for overturning the 'quick fix' testing mentality that is cheaper but does not serve creative capacity assessment at all well. With creative capacity being a complex set of dispositions, high-level aptitudes and unique lifestyle preferences, one-hit tests or skills or personality or aptitudes will not serve in themselves as credible evidence of a creative worker potential.

That said, it is worth noting the changes being made to one-off employer test instruments to pick up on creative dispositions and propensities. Microsoft's test paper contains a number of thinking challenges that shift the emphasis from probing generic competencies or personality traits to focus squarely on innovative problem-solving.[33] This approach to assessment exemplifies the approach of many employers who are less and less interested in school or university results and more and more interested in evidence of a potential employee's capacity to think. Some examples of how Microsoft tests thinking, not schooling, are provided in example 8.5.

Example 8.5 Microsoft employment aptitude test samples

Question: If a bear walks one mile south, turns left and walks one mile to the east and then turns left again and walks one mile north and arrives at its original position, what is the color of the bear?

Answer: The color of the bear is trivial. The possible solutions to it are interesting. In addition to the trivial North Pole, there are additional circles near South Pole. Think it out.

Question: Given a rectangular (cuboidal for the puritans) cake with a rectangular piece removed (any size or orientation), how would you cut the remainder of the cake into two equal halves with one straight cut of a knife?

Answer: Join the centers of the original and the removed rectangle. It works for cuboids too! BTW, I have been getting many questions asking why a horizontal slice across the middle will not do. Please note the 'any size or orientation' in the question! Don't get boxed in by the way you cut your birthday cake :) Think out of the box.

Problem: There are three baskets. One of them has apples, one has oranges only and the other has mixture of apples and oranges. The labels on their baskets always lie (i.e. if the label says oranges, you are sure that it doesn't have oranges only, it could be a mixture). The task is to pick one basket and pick only one fruit from it and then correctly label all the three baskets.

HINT: There are only two combinations of distributions in which ALL the baskets have wrong labels. By picking a fruit from the one labeled MIX-TURE, it is possible to tell what the other two baskets have.
Problem: Why is a manhole cover round?
HINT: The diagonal of a square hole is larger than the side of a cover!
Alternate answers: 1. Round covers can be transported by one person, because they can be rolled on their edge. 2. A round cover doesn't need to be rotated to fit over a hole.[34]

It is also worth noting that, just as Microsoft's tests mark a very different approach to job performance criteria, so too the Microsoft 'personality inventory' has a different take from the more predictable personality tests such as those that cling to the 'Big Five' personality dimensions (Extraversion, Emotional Stability, Agreeableness, Conscientiousness and Openness to Experience)[35] or to the identification of certain psychological differences according to typological theories such as the Myers-Briggs Personality test. While some of their 'personality test' questions may still be relatively predictable in any future employment scenario (such as employee expectations, resumé clarification and prior knowledge of the organisation), others are less so. These probes (for example, what is your ideal working environment? Why do you think you are smart? What is your geographical preference?) are more reflective of Richard Florida's emphasis on talent, tolerance and technology (the last implied by the fact of an application to Microsoft) as well as his interest in the 'new geography of class'.[36]

Less calculation, more integration

However we go about assessing creative capacity, we will be best served by an approach that can integrate many of the principles that underpin the research, trials and example presented in this chapter. This means actively directing and supporting young people in the on-going self-management of their own assessment package. They need to become familiar with the affordances of a wide range of instruments, activities and technology that can be used to assemble and edit evidence of their performance and their learning, including peer-to-peer assessment, self-assessment, their capacity to design creative solutions, to articulate key moments in their creative work and to demonstrate that they have been – and are – agile and innovative thinkers and doers.

To meet the requirements of the creative workforce, no self-assessment package or portfolio can stand alone, nor can it remain static. There can be no template for making a one-size-fits-all portfolio. Useful portfolios will need to be as dynamic as the creative lifestyle and work culture they are meant to impress. They will therefore need to reflect a capacity to utilise the latest digital tools in their constantly changing design. It is not a matter of leaving academic credentials behind, nor is it a matter of stepping around the added assessment requirements of a particular business organisation. It is a matter of integrating all as credible evidence that, in terms of creative capacity, our future creatives can and do measure up.

9

Over the horizon

Anticipating the future, like creativity, is everyone's business. To that extent, we all need to think like futurists when it comes to preparing creative workers. Thinking like futurists is not about ignoring the past but learning from it.

The future will continue to surprise us. This, according to control theorist William Gosling, occurs when we find that the future is neither more of the same nor a gradual process of improvement or decline but the sort of transformational change that he calls the 'knight's move'.[1] Many of our predictions from the past turned out to be wrong: the millennium bug, the paperless office, more leisure time and so on. Yet there are crucial changes we did not predict: how email would reshape our work, how the internet would create a very different social and commercial world, how much time young people would spend texting each other, how a Stanley knife could be used as a weapon of mass destruction.

When we look at the concerns that professional educators have had at different times about the future, many of their dire predictions about the negative influence of technology on young people now seem to us to be ludicrous. America's National Association of Teachers records that:

- In 1703 teachers worried that students who used slate rather than preparing bark would run out of slate.
- By 1815 teachers worried that students were too dependent on paper instead of slate, and that this would mean disaster if and when the paper ran out.
- In 1917 teachers worried that students depended far too much on ink and had forgotten how to sharpen their pencils with a knife.
- By 1928 teachers complained that students depended far too much on store-bought ink and had – disastrously – forgotten how to make their own.
- Ball point pens were not acceptable to academics in 1955 – fountain pens only were to be used when submitting papers.
- Concerns that slide rules would eliminate problem-solving skills emerged in the 1960s.
- By 1980 panic had set in around the numerical skills being lost because of the advent of the pocket calculator.[2]

The fact that these predictions seem laughable in retrospect is good reason for us to question the reasons we give today for being a nay-sayer in relation to change. What we can learn from three centuries of nay-saying is that there is a long and strong educational tradition of fearing rather than embracing a future in which technological innovation is a key player.

In an age that is increasingly dependent on, and ignorant of, science and technology,[3] revisiting the fears and panics of the past prompts us to imagine what we might make of our present educational fears in the next few decades: fears that SMS-ing will be detrimental to young people's capacity to spell; fears that kids won't get a job because they don't understand what 'next-of-kin' means on a job application form; fear that kids will lose the capacity to remember facts because they are so fast at finding them; fears that kids who engage too much with games will be unemployable.

This is where it gets tricky because we cannot simply dismiss these fears by claiming that the obverse is true – that traditional literacy and numeracy won't matter, that memory won't matter, or that a high level of game-playing will mean future social success. We need to negotiate a pathway rather than take a fixed position on what the future holds and what it means.

Futurist thinking is not, therefore, about giving three cheers for digital technology. Nor is it about inventing doomsday scenarios about its sinister potentials, despite the fact that many of those who have touted both extremes have been rewarded with commercial success. Whatever we use to develop creative capacity in ourselves and others, we know that technological affordances come wrapped in barbed wire. Knowing this, we are able to move to a position of informed 'yea saying' in relation to the possibilities that new technology affords those 21st-century learners who become creative workers.

Negotiating creative futures

Our education systems have been very much supply-led; our entertainment has been very much demand-led. This has meant, among other things, that the values that we think our young people ought to have, and the things they might actually want to, are contested. Community leaders, educators and parents worry about the sort of capacity they should have and who ought to be in charge of developing them. There are fears that entertainment has had too much power in determining values that should be formed in local communities under the watchful eye of those who 'know better'. Meanwhile, young people continue to form their identities and social networks out of the playful and experimental cultures that new technology affords, for better and worse.

The Yuk/Wow Generation is an 'experience' generation, so they may well take experimentation to extremes: witness binge-drinking, 'tomb-stoning' (the dangerous practice of diving off high places such as bridges and buildings), swarming and other potentially dangerous or anti-social behaviour. These practices contrast markedly with the things they consider to be 'sooooo boring' about their lives, and that generally includes their experiences of formal schooling.

It needs to be said, however, that most young people – if often bored by the curriculum, pedagogy and assessment of schooling itself – are pretty forgiving of their teachers, whose lot, they know, is not a happy one. Many have good relationships with individual teachers and very much enjoy the social life they have at school, so much so that often they can't wait for holidays to end to return to friends and the buzz of their social networks. Put simply, they know how mass custody works and what is in it for them.

They also know that there is a 'real world' out there. It is typical of the thinking of young people – and indeed many teachers and academics – that the real world exists where they ain't. So the real world is university – until they get to university. Then the real world becomes the world in which they can afford to live their preferred lifestyle. Many do taste the reality of a McDonald's job, but undergraduates aspire to more than this: a better salary, more autonomy, more flexibility, cool people to be with, a cool place to live. For the Yuk/Wows, the ideal reality is cool.

In the twenty-first century compelling questions arise around the future of the entire workforce, not just the creative workforce to which many of the Yuk/Wows aspire. Will the majority of young people have any sort of meaningful work, and how would non-participation affect them? As Jeremy Rifken, author of *The End of Work*, sees it, the most likely long-term future is that only about a fifth of the current workforce will be in employment.[4] This is despite the cushioning effect of training, short-term job compacts and the like. Most of our young people, then, will need to forge new identities that have meaning and dignity independent of an occupation or workplace.

Already we are seeing the blurring of distinctions like 'workplace' and 'home', so it is realistic to presume that we will see more blurring of the idea of work being bound by time and place. New patterns of work are changing the structure of household living, as work intensifies, requiring more mobility, more home-based communication technology and 24/7 responsiveness. According to Barbara Pocock, director of the Centre for Life and Work at the University of South Australia, traditional work/home configurations are being disrupted by the newly emergent workforce cultures. She says that workers and those they live with are now looking for 'new ways to save time, form and sustain relationships, work, live, and care for each other',[5] and this has implications for a whole raft of community issues, including sustainable living and the planning of new urban developments.

One of the positive affordances of high levels of creative capacity is agility in relation to occupation and location. This means that it allows for – indeed encourages – the development of an identity that is for living, not just working. Instead of being destabilised by the temporary or permanent loss of paid full-time employment, a young person with the resources that creativity brings can still be meaningfully engaged in their social and community networks. Creative capacity-building – that is, learning to be more imaginative and original, learning to explore for the purpose of discovery, seeing unusual connections, using and combining thinking skills and communicating well – can make for a rich and rewarding future both within and outside the workplace.

Of course it is easy to become romantic about what creativity can offer when there is no milk in the fridge – indeed, when there is no fridge! What is important here is that the skills of self-management acquired throughout the learning journey can assist young people to generate their own future, by creating employment opportunities that currently do not exist and by improving on all those products and practices that are unsustainable for the planet.

A more recent and perhaps less gloomy prognosis is provided in the summary of outcomes of the 2005 World Congress on the Future of Work.[6] The authors concluded, among other things, that the future of work will be determined as much by communities as by companies, so one of the biggest challenges will be 'the degree and kind of control that individual workers have over where when and what they do to produce value'.[7] This means serious renegotiation of who is in charge of what and when. If more workers choose to do personal business in business hours and business in 'after' hours, then there are implications for CEOs who want to keep '9-to-5' control.

As a corollary to this, they anticipate that 'corporate offices and will undergo radical redesign as architects and facilities managers redefine their roles as enablers of work, not as creators and managers of physical spaces'. This will require a radical shift in the social roles and competencies needed by professionals. Managers of facilities will not be able to focus solely on the infrastructure and its maintenance but will need to engage closely with the needs of the people for optimal productivity. The bean-counters, bureaucrats and budget boys will be seriously challenged in this new order of things.

The 'new order of things' in the workplace will be responsive to larger global shifts that will affect everyone regardless of where they are located or how they choose to live their lives. The Institute for the Future, based in California, has for fifty years been involved in the work of mapping these global shifts, based on the assumption that the future will be a variation of themes from our past. Their Map of the Decade (2006–16) elaborates on six of these themes – Markets, Practices, Tools, People, Places and Ecologies.[8] Their predictions include the following:

→ *More people go creative.* People will spend more time creating and consuming their own personal media, and will be able to take this 'rich and compelling world' wherever they go, through geoblogging that links the personal media world with real-world locations. They will also engage actively in personal reinvention as they confront the new global challenges of environmental socioeconomic change.

→ *Things start to get smart.* Data, sensors and semantic processing will increasingly be embedded into things, people and places. This will not look like the robotic world so often envisaged in fiction but 'more like an exquisite dance between groups of people and the spaces they occupy'.

→ *New business models make what was previously profitable now virtually free.* The global marketplace will be changed by the diffusion of distributed lightweight infrastructure technology, causing the resources of heavy infrastructure players to become unprofitable.

↳ *The first generation of internet kids enter the workforce* with their new tools, social practices and values. The predilection of this new generation for group and collective behaviour, plus their distinctively branded individualism, will have a powerful influence on workplace governance. As a result, we will see different management structures and different forms of reward and recognition.

These predictions take us only a few years away from where we are now. What happens if we try to look beyond 2016? Rodney Hill, futurist at the University of Texas, tells us that, by 2017, our iPods will contain the US Library of Congress. He names the following as educators' 'complaints of the future':

↳ 2023 complaint: 'They have implanted the Library of Congress in their heads. What are we supposed to teach them now?'

↳ 2025 complaint: 'The internet implant in the brain has been refined. How will that affect college entrance scores?'

↳ 2030 complaint: 'How can you tell which students are natural humans and which are enhanced genetically and/or through artificial intelligence?'

↳ 2040 complaint: 'They have given me a mixed class of humans, hybrids and transhumanists. How do I deal with the various learning styles?'⁹

I have not tried to respond to Hill's predictions, although these scenarios may well be upon us sooner than we suspect. They seem bizarre to us, as bizarre perhaps as the teacher complaints of the last three centuries seem ludicrous. We are no different from our predecessors in being anxious about the future, nor in wanting the very best for the young people who will be the future.

What that 'very best' will be is not just something simply to be hoped for but something that has to be brought into being. A recent edited collection, *Creativity, Wisdom and Trusteeship*, distils some of the thoughts of leading educators about how that should happen.[10] Helen Haste, for example, names five 'key competencies' needed for 21st-century living that are aligned with much that has been written in earlier chapters of this book. They are: the ability to manage ambiguity and diversity; the ability to embrace agency and responsibility; the ability to find and sustain community; the ability to manage emotion; and technological competence.[11] Guy Claxton once again stresses the importance of wisdom – of perspicacity, disinterestedness and empathy – in augmenting what has often been left out of discussions of the 'creative' disposition.[12] For Jonathan Rowson, what is paramount is the capacity to engage with the complexity of the way that motivation, values, habit and freedom interact.[13]

All this is deliberate, important and unfinished work. It is not about nailing down the debates or developing the right formula for preparing to build creative capacity. Rather the point is to keep ideas in play, to live with the tensions that will continue to arise as the times become more complex and the requisite skills and dispositions become a bigger and more demanding wish list. Complexity is a condition we have to live with, in the knowledge that not all problems are amenable to solution. The sudden 'breakthrough' – of Eureka moments in a bath, of instant discovery – is as mythical as the notion that creativity is all about individual genius. Problems are solved by hard work and persistence – by moving away from falsity, not moving towards the Truth. We learn more from failed experiments than from confirming ones. So the disposition to serious play, to deep and respectful engagement with unfamiliar things and people, to enjoy crossing boundaries, to seek out challenges and to be constructively self-critical – all this will serve the Yuk/Wow Generation better than any disposition born of regimes of compliance and control.

The next generation of workers will not solve all the thorny problems we have left them, but hopefully they will make a better fist of engaging with complexity than we have done. Meanwhile there is no more important work in the present than to enable our young people to have fulfilling, ethical and creative futures.

Notes

1 Creativity is everyone's business

1 Greene, R (2007), 'A model of 42 models of creativity', <http://musicalcreativity.com/?p=16>, viewed 11 April 2008.

2 See McWilliam, E, & Dawson, S (2007), *Understanding Creativity: A Survey of 'Creative' Academic Teachers: A Report Produced for the Carrick Institute for Learning and Teaching in Higher Education*, <www.carrickinstitute.edu.au/carrick/webdav/site/carricksite/users/siteadmin/public/fellowships_associatefellow_report_ericamcwilliam_may07.pdf>, viewed 11 April 2008.

3 Johnson, P (2006), *Creators: From Chaucer to Walt Disney*, London: HarperCollins.

4 See McWilliam & Dawson, *Understanding Creativity*.

5 Slattery, L (2007), 'Creation theories', *Australian Literary Review*, 3 October 2007, p. 20.

6 Weisberg, R (1999), 'Creativity and knowledge', in R Sternberg (ed.), *Handbook of Creativity*, Cambridge: Cambridge University Press, pp. 226–50.

7 McWilliam & Dawson, *Understanding Creativity*.

8 See Mark Hobart's (1993) edited collection, *An Anthropological Critique of Development: The Growth of Ignorance*, London: Routledge, for a fuller treatment of the nature of developmental knowledge.

9 Email from james@impactfactory.com.au, received 19 February 2008.

10 Vitebsky, P (1993), 'Is death the same everywhere? Contexts of knowing and

doubting', in Hobart (ed.), *An Anthropological Critique of Development*, p. 100.

11   Claxton, G (2006), 'Creative glide space', in C Bannerman (ed.), *Navigating the Unknown: The Creative Process in Contemporary Performing Arts*, London: Middlesex University Press, p. 1.

12   See McWilliam & Dawson, *Understanding Creativity*.

13   Florida, R (2003), *The Rise of the Creative Class*, Melbourne: Pluto Press.

14   <www.coolcities.com/cm/attach/ACFAEF2D-708B-4861-96D4-CA6FD5B87436/Creative_Class_economic_dev_RFlorida.pdf>, viewed 21 April 2008.

15   Ibid.

16   Ibid.

17   See for instance T Nichols Clark (2002), 'Urban amenities: Lakes, opera and juice bars: Do they drive development?', <www.coolcities.com/cm/attach/ACFAEF2D-708B-4861-96D4-CA6FD5B87436/UrbanAmenitiesandGrowthUC.pdf>, viewed 21 April 2008.

18   Jacobs, K, 'Why I don't love Richard Florida', <www.metropolismag.com/cda/story.php?artid=1151>, viewed 14 February 2008.

19   Ibid., p. 13.

20   For example, see the exploration of peripatetic academic life by McWilliam, E, Bridgstock, R, Lawson, A, Evans, T, & Taylor, PG (2008), 'Who's Dean today? Acting and interim management as paradoxes of the contemporary university', in *Higher Education Policy and Management* 30(3):323–35.

21   McGill, C, & Elliott, S (2004), *Wine Dogs: The Dogs of Australasian Wineries*, Rozelle, NSW: Giant Dog Pty Ltd.

22   C Barnett, Intel chairman, cited in Haring-Smith, T (2007), 'Creativity as a goal for student learning', Keynote Address, 2007 PKAL Summer Institute, Project Kaleidoscope, p. 2.

23   Hearn, G (2007), *If Your Company Were a Cockroach: How to Survive in the New Business Ecology*, Brisbane: Queensland University of Technology, pp. 3–4.

24   Ibid., p. 6.

25   *Cox Review of Creativity in Business*, cited on Creativity: Innovation and Industry Conference, <http://cii.dmu.ac.uk>, viewed 11 April 2008.

26   See Edward de Bono, <www.edwdebono.com>, viewed 11 April 2008.

27   See for example Schirrmacher, R (2005), *Art and Creative Development for Young Children*, Albany, NY: Delmar Thomson Learning.

28   Csikszentmihalyi, M (2006), 'Foreword: Developing creativity', in N Jackson, M Oliver, M Shaw, J Wisdom (eds), *Developing Creativity in Higher Education: An Imaginative Curriculum*, London: Routledge, p. xviii.

29   Jackson, N (2006), 'Imagining a different world', in Jackson et al. (eds), *Developing Creativity in Higher Education*, p. 8.

30   See Fletcher, A (2001), *The Art of Looking Sideways*, London: Phaidon Press, for these and other comments on creativity from practising artists.

31   Amabile, TA, Hadley, CN, & Kramer, SJ (2002), 'Creativity under the gun', *Harvard Business Review*, August, pp. 52–61.

32   Taraborrelli, JR (2003), *Michael Jackson: The Magic and the Madness*, London: Pan Macmillan, p. 240.

33   See Tepper, S (2006), 'Taking the measure of the creative campus', *Peer Review*, 8(2), at <www.aacu.org/peerreview/pr-sp06/pr-sp06_analysis1.cfm>, viewed 21 April 2008.

34 Bowkett, S (2005), *100 Ideas for Teaching Creatively*, London: Continuum.
35 Rorty, R (1989), *Contingency, Irony and Solidarity*, New York: Cambridge University Press.
36 Haraway, D (1991), *Simians, Cyborgs and Women: The Reinvention of Nature*, London: Free Association Books, p. 149.
37 Koestler, A (1964), *The Act of Creation*, New York: Macmillan, p. 95.
38 Perkins, D (1981), *The Mind's Best Work*, Cambridge, MA: Harvard University Press.
39 Meredith, S, & Francis, D (2000), 'Journey towards agility: The agile wheel explored', *TQM Magazine*, 12(2): 138.
40 Inkson, K, & Parker, P (2005), 'Boundary-less careers and the transfer of knowledge: A 'Middle Earth' perspective', *Higher Education Policy*, 18: 313–25.

2 The Yuk/Wow Generation

1 Beck, JC, & Wade, M (2006), *The Kids are Alright: How the Gamer Generation is Changing the Workplace*, Boston: Harvard Business School Press, p. xiv.
2 Ibid., p. xv.
3 Mackay, H (2007), *Advance Australia Where? How We've Changed, Why We've Changed and What Will Happen Next*, Sydney: Hachette Australia, p. 61.
4 Ibid.
5 Howkins, J (2002), *The Creative Economy: How People Make Money from Ideas*, London: Penguin.
6 Ibid., pp. 155–8.
7 *Ipswich Girls' Grammar Magazine*, November 1938, pp. 13–14.

3 The creative workforce

1 Cited by K Byron (2007), 'A view from the outside', keynote address presented at Creativity or Conformity: Building Cultures of Creativity in Higher Education (conference), Cardiff University, 8–10 January.
2 Bradley, IC (1976), *The Call to Seriousness: The Evangelical Impact on the Victorians*, New York: Macmillan, p. 51.
3 Toffler, A (1970), *Future Shock*, London: Pan Books, p. 362.
4 Ibid.
5 Steiny, J (2007), 'Our factory-model schools are soul-killers for students', <www.redorbit.com/news/education/1178638/our_factorymodel_schools_are_soulkillers_for_students/index.html>, viewed 21 April 2008.
6 Devine, M (2006), 'Creativity in the world of work', *Peer Review*, 8(2), <www.aacu.org/peerreview/pr-sp06>, viewed 14 April 2008.
7 Florida, R, & Goodnight, J (2005), 'Managing for creativity', *Harvard Business Review*, 83(7/8): 124–31.
8 See, for example, the special Spring 2006 issue of *Peer Review* (Vol. 8, No. 2) for a number of articles elaborating the theme 'The Creative Imperative'.
9 Castells, M (2001), *The Internet Galaxy*, Oxford: Oxford University Press.
10 Sassen, S (2004), 'Saskia Sassen: Space and power', in N. Gane (ed.), *The Future of Social Theory*, Continuum: London, pp. 125–42.
11 Quiggan, J (2007), 'Innovation begins at home', paper presented at Digital

Literacy and Creative Innovation in a Knowledge Economy (symposium), Queensland State Library, South Bank, 29–30 March.

12 Howkins, *The Creative Economy*.

13 Cunningham, S, Cutler, T, Hearn, G, Ryan, MD, Keane, M (2005), 'From "culture" to "knowledge": An innovation systems approach to the content industries', in C Andrew, M Gattinger, MS Jeannotte, W Straw (eds), *Accounting for Culture: Thinking Through Cultural Citizenship*, Ottawa: University of Ottawa Press, pp. 104–23.

14 Economic Review Committee (ERC; 2002), *Singapore's Creative Industries Development Strategy*, Ministry of Trade and Industry, 25 September. See <www.mti.gov.sg/public/ERC/frm_ERC_Default.asp?sid=131>.

15 ARC Centre of Excellence for Creative Industries and Innovation (CCi) (2005), *CDI National Mapping Project*, <https://wiki.cci.edu.au/display/NMP/NMP+Home>, viewed 14 April 2008.

16 See <https://wiki.cci.edu.au/display/NMP/NMP+home>, viewed 14 April 2008.

17 Statistics quoted by Edna Del Santos in her keynote speech to the China Beijing International High-tech Expo, Beijing, June 2007.

18 Howkins, *The Creative Economy*.

19 <www.abc.net.au/news/stories/2007/03/06/1863865.htm>, viewed 14 April 2008.

20 Binder, A (2006), *Preparing America's Workforce: Are We Looking in the Rear-View Mirror?* Working Paper, Centre for Economic Policy, Princeton University.

21 Ibid., p. 2.

22 Cited in Wince-Smith, DL (2006), 'The creativity imperative: A national perspective', *Peer Review*, 8(2), <www.aacu.org/peerreview/pr-sp06/pr-sp06_analysis3.cfm>, 21 April 2008.

23 Brown, P, Hesketh, A, & Williams, S (2002), 'Employability in a knowledge-driven economy', *Journal of Education and Work*, 16(2): 107–26.

24 Yorke, M (2006), *Employability in Higher Education: What It Is – What It is Not*, Learning and Emplyability Series 1, UK Higher Education Academy, April.

25 Ibid., p. 5.

26 NCEE (2007), *Tough Choices or Tough Times: The Report of the New Commission on the Skills of the American Workforce*, National Center on Education and the Economy, <www.skillscommission.org>, p. 5.

27 Ibid., p. 7.

28 Department of Science, Education and Training (DEST) (2002), *Employability Skills for the Future*, Canberra: Commonwealth of Australia.

29 Varina Nissen, cited in Taylor, M (2005), 'Bosses' wishlist a problem being solved', *Age*, 30 July, p. 12.

30 Australian Industry Group and Allen Consulting Group (2006), *World Class Skills for World Class Industries: Employers' Perspectives on Skilling in Australia*, <www.aigroup.asn.au>, p. 16.

31 Beck & Wade, *The Kids are Alright*.

32 Ibid., p. 2.

33 Oblinger, D, & Oblinger, J (2005), Understanding the Net Generation (Educause e-book), p.2.8, <www.educause.edu/content.asp?PAGE_

ID=5989&bhcp=1>, viewed 21 April 2008.

34 Amabile, TA, Hadley, CN, & Kramer, SJ (2002), 'Creativity under the gun', *Harvard Business Review*, August, p. 52.

35 Ibid., pp. 55–6.

36 Martin, B. (2007), *Building and Sustaining a Culture of Leadership*, Keynote presentation at the 13th International Conference on Thinking, Norrkoping, Sweden, 18 June.

37 Wilmot, B (2007), 'Hot property', *Boss Magazine* 8 (special issue: *Reinventing Leadership*), p. 69, <www.afrboss.com.au>.

38 Ibid.

39 Chesterton, GK (1909), *Orthodoxy*, New York: Lane Press (republished 1974, Greenwood Press, Westport), pp. 149–50.

40 Ericson, RV, & Haggerty, KD (1997), *Policing the Risk Society*, Toronto: University of Toronto Press, p. 104.

41 Buckingham, M, & Coffman, C (2000), *First, Break All the Rules*, New York: Simon & Schuster.

42 Ibid., p. 57.

4 Education: important and irrelevant

1 See for example the World Bank Policy Research Working Paper 4122 (February 2007), which amasses empirical evidence to show that a strong relationship exists worldwide between educational quality and economic growth.

2 NCEE, *Tough Choices or Tough Times*, p. 6.

3 Warschauer, M (2007), 'The paradoxical future of digital learning', *Learning Inquiry*, 1: 1–49.

4 Bolter, JD (1991), *Writing Space: The Computer, Hypertext and the History of Writing*, Hillsdale, NJ: Lawrence Erlbaum Associates.

5 Attewell, P, & Winston, H (2003), 'Children of the digital divide', in P Attewell & NM Seel (eds), *Disadvantaged Teens and Computer Technologies*, Munster, Germany: Waxmann, pp. 117–36.

6 Warschauer, 'The paradoxical future of digital learning', p. 43.

7 OECD (2006), *Results from Programme for International Student Assessment* (PISA) 2003, compiled by Andreas Schleicher, OECD Directorate for Education.

8 Kennedy, G, Krause, K, Judd, T, Churchward, A, & Gray, K (2006), *First Year Students' Experiences with Technology: Are They Really Digital Natives?* Preliminary Report of Findings, September, Centre for Study of Higher Education, University of Melbourne.

9 Katz, R (2005) in Kvavik, R, & Caruso, J (eds), *ECAR Study of Students and Information Technology*, <www.educause.edu/ir/library/pdf/ers0506/rs/ERS0506w.pdf>, viewed 27 April 2008.

10 Kennedy et al., *First Year Students' Experiences with Technology*, p. 16.

11 NCEE, *Tough Choices or Tough Times*, pp. 6–7.

12 Pink, DH (2005), *A Whole New Mind*, New York: Penguin.

13 Robinson, K (2007), 'The other climate crisis: Digital culture, demography and education', keynote address to Digital Literacy and Creative Innovation in a Knowledge Economy (research symposium), 29–30 March, Queensland

State Library, Brisbane.

14 Ipsos MORI (2007), *Student Expectations Study: Key Findings from Online Research and Discussion Evenings Held in June 2007 for the Joint Information Systems Committee*, p. 16, <http://connect.educause.edu/Library/Abstract/StudentExpectationsStudy/45255>, viewed 27 April 2008.

15 Beck, U (1992) *Risk Society: Towards a New Modernity*, London: Sage.

16 Florida, R (2004), 'The rise of the creative class', keynote address, sponsored by the Homery Institute, Roundhouse Theatre, Kelvin Grove Urban Village, Brisbane, 22 March.

17 Florida, *The Rise of the Creative Class*, p. 249.

18 Overland, M (2007), 'Restricted room for creativity', *Australian Higher Education Supplement*, 31 October, p. 36.

19 Robinson, 'The other climate crisis'.

20 Claxton, G (2004), *Learning is Learnable (and We Ought to Teach It)*, <www.guyclaxton.com/documents/New/Learning%20Is%20Learnable.pdf>, viewed 15 April 2008.

21 Warschauer, 'The paradoxical future of digital learning', p. 46.

22 See McWilliam, E, & Perry, L (2006), 'On being more accountable: The push and pull of risk in school leadership', *International Journal of Educational Leadership*, 9(2): 97–110.

23 Mulcahy, D, cited in Brenneis, D, Shore, C, & Wright, S (2003), 'Audit culture and the politics of accountability: The price of bureaucratic peace', paper presented at the Presidential Panel of AAA, Chicago, 21 November, p. 7.

24 See for example Ranson, S (2003), 'Public accountability in the age of neo-liberal governance', *Journal of Education Policy*, 18(5): 459–80. See also Lingard R et al. (2002), *Addressing the Educational Needs of Boys*, Canberra: Department of Education, Science and Training.

25 Warschauer, 'The paradoxical future of digital learning', p. 42.

26 Blinder, A (2006), *Preparing America's Workforce: Are We Looking in the Rearview Mirror?* Princeton University Center for Economic Policy Studies, CEPS Working Paper No. 135, October.

27 Bauman, Z, cited by Gane, N (2004), 'Zigmunt Bauman: Liquid sociality', in Gane, *The Future of Social Theory*, Continuum: London, pp. 17–46.

28 Ibid., p. 21.

29 The other four are: the Healthy Citizen, the Informed Citizen, the Democratic Citizen and the Eco-Citizen.

30 Queensland Government (2008), 'What state schools value: Active and informed citizens for a sustainable world', <http://education.qld.gov.au/curriculum/docs/what-state-schools-value.doc>, viewed 23 April 2008.

31 Kennedy et al., *First Year Students' Experiences with Technology*.

32 Ibid., p. 3.

33 OECD (2006), *Results from Programme for International Student Assessment (PISA) 2003*, compiled by Andreas Schleicher, OECD Directorate for Education.

34 Ibid.

35 Csikszentmihalyi, M. (1999), 'Implications of a systems perspective for the study of creativity', in R Sternberg (ed.), *Handbook of Creativity*, Cambridge: Cambridge University Press, pp. 313–35.

36 Sinclair, A (1992), 'The tyranny of a team ideology', *Organisation Studies*, 13(4): 611–26.

37 See Lave, J (1993), 'Situating learning in communities of practice', in LB Resnick, JM Levine & SD Teasley (eds), *Perspectives on Socially Shared Cognition*, Washington, DC: American Psychological Association, pp. 17–36. See also Lave, J, & Wenger, E (1991), *Situated Learning: Legitimate Peripheral Participation*, Cambridge: Cambridge University Press.

38 See Thompson, K (2006), 'Enhance team performance by consistent individual behaviour', <www.bioteams.com/2006/03/22/enhance_team_performance.html>, viewed 15 April 2008.

5 Teacher: sage, guide, meddler

1   McKenzie, J (2001), excerpt from 'The wired classroom', <http://members.shaw.ca/priscillatheroux/teacherrole.html>, viewed 15 April 2008.

2   Ibid., p. 1.

3   <http://en.wikipedia.org./wiki/Freddie_Mercury>, viewed 15 April 2008.

4   <www.blueman.com/about/whatis>, viewed 15 April 2008.

5   See <www.nintendo.com/wii>, viewed 15 April 2008.

6   <www.blueman.com/news>, viewed 24 December 2007, p. 1.

7   Ibid., p. 3.

8   Seely Brown, J (2006), 'New learning environments for the twenty-first century', *Change*, 6(5): 2.

9   Brun, A (2006), 'Teaching the produsers: Preparing students for user-led content production', ATOM Conference, Brisbane, 8 October; <http://snurb.info/node/604>, viewed 15 April 2008.

10 Seely Brown, 'New learning environments for the twenty-first century', p. 2.

11 Prensky, M (2002), 'The motivation of game play: The real 21st-century learning revolution', *On the Horizon* 10(1): 5–11.

12 Ibid., p. 6.

13 Cited in OECD (2007), *Understanding the Brain: The Birth of a Learning Science*, OECD Centre for Education Research and Innovation, p. 27.

14 Alberts, B (2005), 'A wakeup call for science faculty', *Cell*, 123: 739–41.

15 See DeHaan, RL (2005), 'The impending revolution in undergraduate science education', *Journal of Science Education and Technology*, 14(2): 253–69.

16 Seely Brown, 'New learning environments for the twenty-first century', p. 2.

17 Rogers, C (1983) in W F O'Neill (ed.), *Re-thinking Education: Selected Readings in the Educational Ideologies*, Iowa: Kendall/Hunt, p. 257.

18 Leadbeater, C (2000), *Living on Thin Air: The New Economy*, New York: Viking.

19 Ibid., p. 4.

20 Claxton, *Learning is Learnable*.

21 Mumford, M, Hunter, S, Eubanks, D, Bedell, K, & Murphy, S (2007), 'Developing leaders for creative efforts: A domain-based approach to leadership development', *Human Resource Management Review*, 17: 404.

22 Ibid.

23 Ibid.

24 Ibid., p. 406.

25 See McWilliam, E (1999), *Pedagogical Pleasures*, New York: Peter Lang

Publishing.

26 Seely Brown, 'New learning environments for the twenty-first century', p. 2.

6 Raising the bar on risk and challenge

1   National Creativity Showcase, Queensland University of Technology, 6–7 December 2007. <www.creativityshowcase.qut.edu.au>, viewed 16 April 2008.
2   These are documented in a DVD of the conference that I, as chair, edited and distributed to conference participants only.
3   Glasser, W (1968), *Schools without Failure*, New York: Harper & Row.
4   See for example Zull, JE (2004), 'The art of changing the brain', *Educational Leadership*, September 2004, 68–72.
5   Claxton, G (2006), 'Expanding the capacity to learn: A new end for education?', opening keynote address, British Educational Research Association Annual Conference, Warwick University, 6 September.
6   Ibid., p. 3.
7   Bruer, J (1999), 'In search of brain-based education', *Phi Delta Kappan*, May, 649–57.
8   Adkins, L, & Lury, C (1999), 'The labour of identity: Performing identities, performing economies', *Economy and Society*, 28(4): 598–614.
9   Rose, N (1990), *Governing the Soul: The Shaping of the Private Self*, London: Routledge.
10 Ibid., p. viii.
11 Ward, S (1996), 'Filling the world with self-esteem: A social history of truth making', *Canadian Journal of Sociology* 2(1): 1–23.
12 Ibid., p. 10.
13 Wilson, D (2000), Foreword, in C Wilson (ed.), *The History of Murder*, New York: Castle Books, p. xix.
14 Dweck, C (1999), *Self-theories: Their Role in Motivation, Personality and Development*, Ann Arbour, MI: Psychology Press.
15 Giddens, A (2002), *Runaway World: How Globalisation is Reshaping Our Lives*, London: Profile Books.
16 Beck, U (1992), *Risk Society: Towards a New Modernity*, London: Sage.
17 Dweck, *Self-theories*, pp. 15–19.
18 Ibid., pp. 16–19.
19 Madero, F (2007), *How to Get the Job You Want*, Sydney: New Holland Publishers.
20 Madero, F (2008), 'Happier New Year', *Courier Mail*, 5–6 January, Career One, p. 3.
21 Ibid.
22 Seely Brown, 'New learning environments for the twenty-first century', p. 2.
23 Claxton, G (2007), 'Wisdom: Advanced creativity?', in A Craft, H Gardiner & G Claxton (eds), *Wisdom, Creativity and Trusteeship*, Thousand Oaks, CA: Corwin Press, p. 43.
24 Claxton, 'Expanding the capacity to learn', p. 2.
25 See, for example, Nickerson, R (1999), 'Enhancing creativity', in RJ Sternberg (ed.), *Handbook of Creativity*, Cambridge: Cambridge University Press, pp. 392–430, and Haring-Smith, T (2006), 'Creativity research review:

Some lessons for higher education', *Peer Review*, 8(2): 23–8.

26 Jenks, C (1996), 'The postmodern child', in J Brannen & M O'Brien (eds), *Children and Families: Research and Policy*, London: Falmer, p. 22.

27 Wallace, J (1997), 'Technologies of "the child": Towards a theory of the child-subject', *Textual Practice*, 9(2): 285–302.

28 Masters, B (1996), *The Evil That Men Do*, London: Black Swan Books, p. 36.

29 Ibid., pp. 36–7.

30 White, J (2006), 'Arias of learning: Creativity and performativity in Australian education', *Cambridge Journal of Education*, 36(3): 435–53.

31 Ibid., pp. 436–47.

32 Masters, *The Evil that Men Do*, pp. 82–6.

33 Bennett, H (2008), 'Tough road to the top', *Weekend Australian*, Career One, p. 1.

34 Bidinost, M (2008), 'Animated by his work', *Age*, My Career, p. 6.

35 Ibid.

7 Flying higher

1 Sudjic, D (2008), 'Designer who gave meaning to everyday objects', *Age*, 10 January, p. 12.

2 Ibid.

3 Pink, DH (2005), *A Whole New Mind*, New York: Penguin.

4 Rossiter, N (2007), 'Report: Creative labour and the role of intellectual property', *Fibreculture*, 1, <http://journal.fibreculture.org/issue1/issue1_rossiter.html>, viewed 16 April 2008.

5 Pink, *A Whole New Mind*, p. 82.

6 Ibid., pp. 100–1.

7 Ibid., p. 111.

8 Robinson, 'The other climate crisis'.

9 Cited in Brenneis, D, Shore, C, & Wright, S (2003), 'Audit culture and the politics of accountability'.

10 Cameron, D (2000), *Good to Talk: Living and Working in a Communication Culture*, London: Sage.

11 See for example Goleman, D (1996), *Emotional Intelligence: Why It Can Matter More Than IQ*, London: Bloomsbury.

12 Kane, P (2004), *The Play Ethic: A Manifesto for a Different Way of Living*, London: Macmillan, p. 63.

13 Ibid., p. 75.

14 Ibid., p. 18.

15 Ibid., p. 62.

16 Pink, *A Whole New Mind*, p. 218.

17 Martin, J (2006), *The Meaning of the Twenty-first Century*, London: Transworld Publishers, pp. 30–2.

18 See Holist Education Network, 'Transdisciplinary inquiry incorporating holistic principles', <www.hent.org/transdisciplinary.htm>, viewed 16 April 2008.

19 Howkins, *The Creative Economy*, p. 7.

20 Ibid.

21 Csikszentmihalyi, M (1999), 'Implications of a systems perspective for the

study of creativity', in R Sternberg (ed.), *Handbook of Creativity*, Cambridge: Cambridge University Press, pp. 313–35.

22   Jackson, N (2006), 'Making sense of creativity in higher education', in Jackson et al. (eds), *Developing Creativity in Higher Education*, pp. 197–230.

23   Stewart, T (1996), 'The great conundrum: You vs the team', *Fortune*, 134(10): 165–6.

24   Seel, R (2006), 'Emergence in organisations', <www.new-paradigm.co.uk/emergence-2.htm>, viewed 17 April 2008.

25   Ibid.

26   See for example SD Dobrev (2005), 'Career mobility and job flocking', *Social Science Research*, 34(4): 800–20.

27   Tosey, P (2006), 'Interfering with the interference: An emergent perspective on creativity in higher education', in Jackson et al. (eds), *Developing Creativity in Higher Education*, p. 31.

28   See C Reynolds (1987), 'Flocks, herds, and schools: A distributed behavioral model', *Computer Graphics* 21(4): 25–34, and Reynolds (1995), 'Boids: Background and update', <www.red3d.com/cwr/boids>, viewed 17 April 2008.

29   Thompson, 'Enhance team performance by consistent individual behaviour'.

30   Ibid.

31   Seel, 'Emergence in organisations'.

32   Thompson, 'Enhance team performance by consistent individual behaviour'.

33   Thompson, K (2006), 'Mass collaboration and virtual crowds', <www.bioteams.com>, viewed 17 April 2008.

34   Ibid.

35   Ibid.

36   See Hof, RD (2005), 'The power of us: Mass collaboration is shaking up business', *Business Week*, 20 June.

37   Seel, 'Emergence in organisations'.

38   See Anderson, C (1998), 'The organisation of foraging in insect societies', PhD thesis, University of Sheffield, and Anderson, C, & Franks, NR (2004), 'Teamwork in ants, robots and humans', *Advances in the Study of Behavior*, 33: 1–48.

39   Dobrev, 'Career mobility and job flocking'.

40   Burt, R (2004), 'Structural holes and good ideas', *American Journal of Sociology*, 110(2): 349–99.

41   Ibid., p. 351.

42   Ibid., p. 353.

43   Ibid., p. 354.

44   Ibid.

45   Ibid., p. 355.

46   Ibid., p. 358.

47   Ibid., p. 390.

48   Ibid.

49   Pidd, C (200), 'Leaders, bosses and bastards: Understanding the Aussie workforce', *Going Public*, Institute of Public Administration, Victoria, pp. 1–4, <www.vic.ipaa.org.au/publications/archive/year/2001>, viewed 23 April 2008.

50   Tosey, 'Interfering with the interference', p. 33.

51 Siemens, G (2005), 'Connectivism: Learning as a network creation', <www.learningcircuits.org/2005/nov2005/seimens.htm>, viewed 17 April 2008.

52 Ibid.

53 OECD (2006), *Twenty-first Century Learning Environments*, Paris: OECD Publishing.

54 Ibid., p. 3.

55 To see this and other design innovations, see OECD, *Twenty-first Century Learning Environments*, pp. 9–49.

8 Measuring up

1   Cited in Howkins, *The Creative Economy*, p. 6.

2   For an elaboration of this history see JF Feldhusen & BE Goh (1995), 'Assessing and accessing creativity: An iterative review of theory, research and development', *Creativity Research Journal*, 8(3): 231–47.

3   Ibid., p. 232.

4   Ibid., pp. 234–5.

5   Ibid., p. 240.

6   Craft, A (2006), 'Creativity in schools', in Jackson et al. (eds), *Developing Creativity in Higher Education*, pp. 19–28.

7   Ibid., p. 27.

8   Moss, P, Girard, B, & Haniford, L (2006), 'Validity in educational assessment', in J Green & A Luke (eds), *Review of Research in Education*, 30: 110.

9   Ibid., p. 112.

10 Cowdroy, R, & de Graff, E (2005), 'Assessing highly creative ability', *Assessment and Evaluation in Higher Education*, 30(5): 511. Original italics.

11 Jackson, N, & Shaw, M (2006), 'Developing subject perspectives on creativity in higher education', in Jackson et al. (eds), *Developing Creativity in Higher Education*, p. 90.

12 See McWilliam & Dawson, *Understanding Creativity*.

13 Oliver, M, Shah, B, McColdrick, C, & Edwards, D (2006), 'Student experiences of creativity', in Jackson et al. (eds), *Developing Creativity in Higher Education*, pp. 43–58.

14 Ibid., p. 47.

15 Ibid., p. 54.

16 McWilliam & Dawson, *Understanding Creativity*.

17 Ibid., pp. 61–4.

18 McWilliam, E, & Dawson, S (in press), 'Teaching for creativity: Towards sustainable and replicable pedagogical practice', *Higher Education*, <www.springerlink.com/content/g518p92082x31221>, viewed 23 April 2008.

19 Jackson, N (2006a), 'Imagining a different world', in Jackson et al. (eds), *Developing Creativity in Higher Education*, p. 3.

20 Ibid., p. 4.

21 Wiles, K (1966), *Historical and Philosophical Foundations of Western Education*, Columbus, OH: Merrill Books, p. 148.

22 See Strathern, M (1997), 'Improving ratings: Audit in the British university system', *European Review*, 5(3): 305–21.

23 Thorndyke, L. (1975) *University Records and Life in the Middle Ages*, New

York: Norton, pp. 3–6.

24 See Asch, E et al. (1998), 'Reinforcement of self-directed learning and the development of professional attitudes through peer and self-assessment', *Academic Medicine*, 73(5): 575.

25 Toohey, S (2002), 'Assessment of students' personal development as part of preparation for professional work – is it desirable and is it feasible?', *Assessment and Evaluation in Higher Education*, 27(6): 529–38.

26 Stables, K, & Kimbell, R (2007), 'Evidence through the looking glass: Developing performance and assessing capability', <www.ep.liu.se/ecp/021/vol1/024/ecp2107024.pdf>, accessed 10 April 2008.

27 Cowdroy, R, & de Graff, E (2005), 'Assessing highly-creative ability', *Assessment and Evaluation in Higher Education*, 30(5): 507–18, <www.informaworld.com/smpp/content~content=a723836755~db=all~order=page>, viewed 27 April 2008.

28 Seely Brown, 'New learning environments for the twenty-first century', pp. 18–25.

29 Ibid., p. 20.

30 Department of Education, Science and Training (2007), *Graduate Employability Skills*, prepared for the Business, Industry and Higher Education Collaboration Council, Commonwealth of Australia, August, <www.dest.gov.au/sectors/higher_education/programmes_funding/programme_categories/key_priorities/business_industry_higher_education_collaboration_council.htm>, viewed 17 April 2008.

31 Ibid., p. 4.

32 Ibid.

33 See <http://halcyon.usc.edu/~kiran/msqs.html>, viewed 23 April 2008.

34 Ibid.

35 <http://psychology.about.com/od/personalitydevelopment/a/bigfive.htm>, viewed 18 April 2008.

36 See Richard Florida summary at <http://creativeclass.org>, 18 April 2008.

9 Over the horizon

1 Gosling, W (1994), *Helmsmen and Heroes: Control Theory as a Key to Past and Present*, London: Weidenfeld & Nicolson.

2 Cited in Hill, R (2007), 'Creativity is the currency of the new millennium', paper presented at Creativity or Conformity: Building Cultures of Creativity in Higher Education (conference), Cardiff, Wales, 8–10 January.

3 Martin, J (2006), *The Meaning of the Twenty-first Century*, London: Transworld Publishers.

4 Rifken, J (2000), *The End of Work: The Decline of the Global Labour Force and the Dawn of the Post-market Era*, New York: Penguin.

5 Pocock, B (2006), *The Configuration of Work, Home and Community in Two Australian Urban Developments: Some Early Analysis*, University of Queensland Workshop Series, 4 August.

6 See <www.thefutureofwork.net/assets/And_a_GoodTime.pdf>, viewed 24 February 2008.

7 Ibid.

8 See <www.kwfdn.org/map/order_copy/order_map.asp> to order a copy of

the map of the decade.

9   Hill, 'Creativity is the currency of the new millennium'.

10   Craft, A, Gardner, H, & Claxton, G (eds) (2008), *Creativity, Wisdom and Trusteeship: Exploring the Role of Education*, Thousand Oaks, CA: Corwin Press.

11   Haste, H (2008), 'Good thinking: The creative and competent mind', in Craft, Gardner & Claxton (eds), *Creativity, Wisdom and Trusteeship*, pp. 96–104.

12   Claxton, G (2008), 'Wisdom: Advanced creativity?', in Craft, Gardner & Claxton (eds), *Creativity, Wisdom and Trusteeship*, pp. 35–48.

13   Rowson, J (2008), 'How are we disposed to be creative?', in Craft, Gardner & Claxton (eds), *Creativity, Wisdom and Trusteeship*, pp. 84–95. Index

Index